ANTHEM PUBLISHING

St. Athanasius: His Life and Times

The Fathers for English Readers

R. Wheler Bush
Headmaster, Marlborough College; Select
Preacher, Oxford

ANTHEM PUBLISHING
Formatted and Printed in the United States of America,
Grand Rapids, MI, Under Whitmer's COVID tyranny.
Entitlement empowers social decay.
Digital edition also available: https://amzn.to/3neKqiC
ISBN: 9798590158683

Editorial Preface

The editorial team at Anthem Publishing has determined that this book represents an important contribution to our knowledge of the Bible and Christian theology. For this reason, we have decided to reissue the book in an affordable paperback and eBook.

We believe that classic scholarship and classic works have a role to play in today's world. We believe classic scholarship can provide much needed perspective on the assumed superiority of modern scholars, and we believe classic treatises transcend the immediate wisdom of the modern world, imparting wisdom that, perhaps, has become unfashionable or difficult to accept.

Additionally, we believe this book as well as the others we publish are a critical part of our cultural identity. We hope that reissuing this book helps to preserve that identity while contributing to Christian theological discussion both today and in the future.

Thank you for purchasing this book from us. We do hope that the book's quality and design meet your standards and that you will find it edifying for many years to come.

—ANTHEM PUBLISHING

CONTENTS

ANTHEM PUBLISHING

St. Athanasius: His Life and Times

The Fathers for English Readers

R. Wheler Bush
Headmaster, Marlborough College;
Select Preacher, Oxford

CHAPTER I
The Birth-Place of Athanasius

Athanasius—the great defender of Christian truth against the heresy of Arius—was bound by the closest ties to Alexandria. In that city he was born, and there he lived and died. The principal events in his checkered career took place there. It was a city which could not fail to exercise a powerful influence on the mind of an intelligent and thoughtful man. Its noble halls and lecture-rooms, its pillared shrine of Serapis, its vast libraries of priceless value, its countless palaces, its broad and far-stretching avenues, its spacious harbours, its immense granaries and docks, its storied pharos, its grand amphitheatre and stadium, its innumerable baths, its motley population, its protecting sea on the north and its wide lake on the south—all these varied and striking objects could not fail to impress any reflective and serious mind with admiration, and to excite the imagination and charm the fancy of all who beheld them. Well did it merit the title of "Beautiful" which was freely bestowed upon it; nor is it wonderful that Ammianus described it as the "crown of all cities," and that Strabo named it the "greatest mart of the world." In the same laudatory style of language Philo, and

Theocritus, and Gregory of Nyssa indulged, when they wrote or spoke of Alexandria.

The attention of Alexander the Great, when he was proceeding along the shore on his journey from Memphis to the shrine of Jupiter Ammon, was, we are told, forcibly arrested by the admirable site for a great city which the sea-coast that lay opposite to the island of Pharos presented. He foresaw how the trade from the East and the West might be concentrated there, and that the situation was eminently fitted to render the city built on that spot the emporium of the commerce of the world. And accordingly, with the promptitude that characterised him, he immediately, with the skilful aid of his architect Dinocrates, proceeded to lay with consummate ability the plan of the city which was to be called after his own name.

The city in which Athanasius lived and had his being stretched for nearly five miles in length from east to west, whilst in depth it scarcely exceeded a single mile. Its figure, therefore, was oblong, and Strabo and Pliny have compared its shape to that of the riding-coat or chlamys worn by the Macedonian cavalry. As was the case in the famous city of Antioch, the principal streets of Alexandria crossed each other rectangularly, and were broad and spacious, some of them being more than 200 feet in width. Two grand avenues adorned with colonnades, along which Athanasius may have often walked, intersected each other, reaching to and from the four main gates of the city. The longer one ran its course of nearly five miles from the great hippodrome on the east to the necropolis on the west; while the shorter one extended from the Gate of the Sun in the south to the Gate of the Moon in the north. The Mediterranean Sea formed the northern boundary-line of the city, and the

Lake Mareotis—whose shores were planted with olives and vines, and where the famous papyrus grew—constituted its southern limit. The island of Pharos sheltered the city from the violence of the Etesian or north winds that swept across the Mediterranean Sea, and the narrow, jutting promontory of Lochias kept off the eastern gales. On the south of the city the Lake Mareotis—the waters of which at one time washed its walls—was connected by many channels of communication with the valley of the Nile and the Red Sea.

We can readily perceive, therefore, that in a strategical point of view, the city was admirably placed. Its harbours—the only serviceable ones from Carthage on the west to Phœnicia on the east—were not only deep, ample in extent, and capable of containing large fleets, but also so formed that they were entered by narrow inlets which could easily be defended. The projecting tongue of land called Lochias, protected by a fort named Acro-Lochias at its extremity, formed one side of the royal port, in which the king's ships of war lay, and where the royal docks, and the palace standing in the midst of trees and gardens, were situated. Between the peninsula of Lochias and the Great Mole (called the "Heptastadium" or seven-furlong bridge) which ran out from the northern line of the city across to the island of Pharos, nearly a mile in length, lay the greater harbour, lined with quays and dockyards; while on the western side of the Mole the harbour formed by this barrier and the island of Pharos, was named the "Haven of Fortunate Return"—*Portus Eunostus*. This harbour was connected with the Great Canal, which led in one direction to the Lake Mareotis, and in the other to the Canopic mouth of the Nile. Along the whole line of the shore from the Temple of Poseidon to the Mole were built the broad granite quays—resembling in some degree the Embankment on the Thames—along which Athanasius might have seen the largest vessels riding at anchor, and finding sufficient depth of water to prevent the necessity of landing in boats. Here, too, he must have noticed the vast warehouses and docks in which were stored the riches of the East and West; and his eye could also have rested at the western end on the famous granaries which rendered Alexandria so important to the Romans. The long, narrow island of Pharos must have often attracted his attention, its white, chalky surface of rock rising up like the white cliffs of our southern coast—a conspicuous object from all parts of the city, the principal houses being so built as to overlook the island and the blue waters of the Mediterranean, while at the eastern extremity of the island the famous lighthouse or pharos, constructed of white marble, at the cost of 800 talents, towered to the height of full 400 feet.

It was a remarkable feature of Alexandria that the city was marked off into three distinct regions, There was first the Egyptian quarter, identical with the site of the old Rhacôtis, where a seafaring community had been gathered together even before the days of Homer ("Od." iv. 355). This quarter was situated at the extreme west of the city. There Athanasius would have gazed with regret, not unmixed with wonder, on the "Serapeium," the magnificent Temple of Serapis— whatever deity Serapis might symbolise or personify— which Dean Milman describes as "the proudest monument of pagan religious architecture next to that of Jupiter in the Capitol," and which Rufinus speaks of as one of the wonders of the world, its architecture combining the grandeur of Egyptian, with the beauty of Grecian, art. There, too, was to be seen the smaller library, called the "Daughter," with its 200,000 volumes.

A second division, occupying the central portion of the city, and standing between the Egyptian quarter on the west, and the Jews' quarter on the east, was called the "Brucheium." This was the royal or Hellenic district, and was the largest in extent. Here could be found the royal palace and the seat of the Roman Government. Here, contiguous to the long central avenue of the city, arose the celebrated library, containing from 400,000 to 700,000 volumes, industriously, perhaps unscrupulously, collected by the kings of the Lagid dynasty—"Elegantiæ regum curæque egregium opus." Here were situated the museum and theatre for lectures, connected with the library by long colonnades of costly marble, and adorned with sphinxes and obelisks carried off from the elder cities of the Pharaohs. The museum, in fact, formed the university of Egypt, where the professors came from every quarter of the world, their professorships being amply endowed by the Ptolemies; and amongst the long array of distinguished men who were either professors or pupils of the museum, some have even named Athanasius himself. In this quarter of the town was to be seen the "Cæsarium," or temple dedicated to the Cæsars; the "Soma"—the mausoleum of the Ptolemies—which was so named from its containing the body of Alexander the Great; the "Dicasterium," or courts of law, the place where, during the dynasty of the Ptolemies, the Senate assembled, and where the "Juridicus" presided under the Romans; the gymnasium, stadium, and amphitheatre, where the games and spectacles so dear to the Alexandrians took place; the "Panium," from whose summit the whole city

was visible; and in the north the Royal Exchange, or
Emporium, where the representatives of every civilised
nation of Europe, Asia, and Africa met for nearly eight
hundred years.

The Jews' quarter constituted the third division of the
city, occupying the eastern extremity of Alexandria.
This quarter would, no doubt, have possessed no little
interest for Athanasius. It had its own walls, its own
Ethnarch, or Arabarches, its own Sanhedrim, and its
own laws. Between the Alexandrian Hellenists and the
Jews frequent and sanguinary contests took place, the
product of religious or political animosities. We learn
from the New Testament (Acts 6:9) that they had their
synagogues for worship, some of whose members are
represented as hotly disputing with Stephen. The effect
of the intermixture of the Greek and the Jew was
remarkable. "Judaism," remarks Dr. Farrar ("Life of St.
Paul," ii. vii.), "was more Hellenised by the contact,
than Hellenism was Judaised." The Jew, brought into
closer contact with the Aryan race, was aroused to wider
sympathies than he had ever felt before.

In this tripartite city Athanasius was thrown into
contact with a mixed and motley multitude, composed
of diverse nationalities congregated together— just such
a multitude as was vividly described by Dion
Chrysostom about seventy years after the
commencement of the Christian era, and portrayed by
Strabo and Polybius. The Alexandrians, especially the
lower orders, were by concurrent opinion regarded as
factious, passionate, untruthful, and cowardly. Their
character was commonly represented as light, frivolous,
sarcastic, and volatile. They were addicted to gambling,
and eagerly devoted to games and shows of every kind.
Such was the opinion that Hadrian formed of them after

his visit to the city ("Vop. Sat.," p. 960). Their fondness for sarcasm and caricature brought down upon them the fierce anger of Caracalla. Their compensating good quality was their thrift and industry. Idleness was unknown amongst them.

For 290 years the Alexandrians were subject to the almost despotic rule of the princes of the Lagid dynasty. During the government of the Romans, when all the highest offices were under the personal control of the Cæsars, Alexandria flourished. The emperors desired to stand well in the estimation of a city which was the great granary of the empire, and many of them visited it.

The ruins of the ancient city now alone bear witness to its former magnificence. Shattered pillars, capitals, obelisks, and statues; masses of masonry which have lost all shape and significance; choked cisterns, fragments of shivered glass and pottery, now alone tell the tale of the city's former grandeur and beauty. The exact ground-plan of the place has been almost irrecoverably lost. The remains of the catacombs of the ancient necropolis at the west gate of the city are of vast extent, cut into the limestone rock that fronts the sea, with which their different chambers communicate. The words of the poet Spenser are singularly apposite:—

> *High towers, fair temples, goodly theatres,*
> *Strong walls, rich porches, princely palaces,*
> *Large streets, brave houses, sacred sepulchres,*
> *Sure gates, sweet gardens, stately galleries,*
> *Wrought with fair pillars and fine imageries;*
> *All these (O pity!) now are turned to dust,*
> *And overgrown with black oblivion's rust.*

But it was not merely outward and material objects that would have appealed to the spirit of such a man as

Athanasius. They would undoubtedly have had their effect. But intercourse with such a population as Alexandria contained must have had its moulding influence upon his cast of thought and on the general tone of his character. His mind must have been enlarged as he was thrown into constant contact with men of almost every nation under heaven, who assembled there for the purpose either of commercial enterprise, or intellectual training, or religious improvement, or theological discussion and research. It was impossible but that a thoughtful mind should have become more reflective, a subtle intellect more acute, a generous and noble nature more wide in its views and more expanded in its sympathies, from association with all the various inhabitants of such an emporium as Alexandria, where commercial speculation, Oriental subtlety, Grecian learning and civilisation, and Roman thoughtfulness, all alike existed;—a "city, which alone of all in the world, has obtained for itself an immortal first-rate name, without violently winning it by the conquests of war, but by purchasing it by the honourable and innocent means of literature and commerce." Such a city and such inhabitants tended to form and mould the mind, the hcart, thc imagination, and the spirit of the great Athanasius. Thus, in addition to the outward surroundings and environment of the distinguished Father of the Church whose life we propose to record, we cannot but perceive that there were other influences of an equally formative character which no less strongly addressed themselves to his intellectual and moral nature. They were influences, moreover, of a peculiar kind, which Alexandria alone of all cities could probably have exerted, and which were traceable to the remarkable character of the philosophy, to the

intellectual development, and to the religious phase of
thought, which prevailed there.

It has been conjectured that the very climate and the
atmospheric condition of Egypt gave a certain bias to
the mind and tone of thought of its educated population.
The peculiar features of the country—the old-world
monuments that met the eye—and the extreme heat
which commonly prevailed, produced a natural
tendency to abstract speculation, to dreamy idealism, to
scholastic refinement and subtlety, to mental analysis,
and to an imaginative and introspective temperament, in
the place of that more vigorous practical philosophy
which a more bracing climate, a colder atmosphere, and
a more mountainous region usually foster. Hence a race
of pure scholars, critics, and idealists sprang up in
Alexandria. The Ptolemies naturally encouraged the
growth and development of the learning and literature
with which they were familiar—a literature which had
ennobled their forefathers, and twined around their
brows a wreath of deathless fame.

The Athenians had carried the Greek language to the
height of perfection. That language had already been
employed to describe every varying phase of thought
and feeling, every philosophical nicety of expression,
every aspect and shade of poetry, every aspiration of
patriotism, every technicality of the law-courts, every
shifting sentiment of the Ecclesia, as well as all the
criticisms of the grammarian, and all the different
notions which the religious controversies, ideas, and
literature of the age had called forth. Such a language,
then, might fairly be supposed to have attained to the
utmost perfection that any form of speech could realise.
Little scope was now left for originality of conception,
for fresh development, or for any further advance in a

healthy, manly, and profitable direction. And consequently the learning that found most commendation and patronage under the Grecian dynasty of kings at Alexandria was of an imitative and ideal character. Its principal occupation was to reproduce the beauties of a language whose prime had now passed. Such a stage of development precluded, for the most part, all really original thought and production. It was consequently an age of verbal speculation, of antiquarian research, of grammatical nicety, of mathematical theory, of refinement and casuistry, rather than of depth, and vigour, and freshness of thought. It gave birth to a mystic and eclectic school of philosophy, such as that of which Ammonius Saccas, in the reign of Severus, became a fashionable exponent. Plato was the great informing mind of that age in philosophy. His views and speculations were combined with the doctrines and terms of the Christian religion, as well as with the theories of the Rabbis, and thus a mixed and composite system was built up, which, instead of improving, really detracted from the distinctive excellences of each several system. With such a philosophy as this—compounded of all the lofty and mysterious language and ideas of Platonism engrafted on the teaching of the Jewish and Christain faith—did the earlier teachers of the gospel at Alexandria endeavour to win over to the truth the educated heathen with whom they were brought into such perpetual contact. For (as we have seen) Alexandria was the nucleus of all the commercial activity of the different nations of the world. Through her port of Berenice and other stations on the Red Sea, the whole Eastern world was thrown open to her influences: by means of the Mediterranean Sea she was brought into close accord with all the more or less civilised nations whose lands were washed by its classic waters; and thus she became a centre towards which all the nations, peoples, and languages of the earth converged.

It would seem probable *a priori* that in a city of such different nationalities and of such varied religions as Alexandria—with a population enlightened by commerce, devoted to the pursuit of literature, and accustomed to the teaching of an eclectic philosophy— the prejudices against the reception of a new religion would not be so great as elsewhere. Moreover, the Jewish portion of the population, which was very large, was not actuated by the same severe and rigorous notions, and the same bigoted views, as it was in many other places, and so would not offer that violent objection to Christianity which many of their more strict brethren elsewhere manifested. The way, too, for the reception of the religion of Christ had been paved by the Septuagint translation of the Scriptures, by means of which translation in the spoken language of the people the knowledge of the One true God had been widely diffused in the city. It is quite possible that Christianity was mixed up with many false views engendered by philosophy, and that its primitive purity and simplicity may have been in some degree dimmed by foreign elements; but it would seem to be certain that many converts were admitted into the Church and baptised, and that a flourishing Christian community was established there. And this is indirectly confirmed by the statements made by Hadrian in a letter which he wrote directly after the visit which he paid to Alexandria.

CHAPTER II
The Birth, Boyhood, and Youth of Athanasius

It seems strange that we have no record of the life of
Athanasius—of what he did and suffered—from the pen
of any of his own particular friends and contemporaries.
The labour, therefore, has fallen upon writers far
removed from his age and generation of separating, in
the story of his life, the chaff from the wheat, of
distinguishing the true from the false, and of
endeavouring to fix in their strict chronological order the
different events in which he was either an actor or a
sufferer.

We cannot look with much confidence on what the
great ecclesiastical historian Eusebius has recorded of
Athanasius. He has, in fact, handed down very little
respecting him, and that little we are unable to accept
without some feeling of distrust, inasmuch as we cannot
but be conscious of Eusebius's known bias and partiality
towards Arianism.

We learn far more from Hilary of his life and doings,
which would be serviceable to the biographer of
Athanasius; but the facts and circumstances which he

adduces are not new and unknown, but have for the most part been recorded by Athanasius himself in his works.

Passing from those who were his more immediate contemporaries, we come to Gregory Nazianzen, who closely followed him; but, from the oratorical cast of his mind which showed itself in his writings, we gain but little accurate, definite, and chronological information in his famous panegyric.

Epiphanius, the contemporary of Gregory, who wrote very fully on the subject of heresy, was biased by Meletian views, and is able to shed but little clear light upon the life of Athanasius.

Rufinus—almost the contemporary of Epiphanius—is justly suspected of carelessness in his narrative of events; and in his chronology is so doubtful, that Socrates, who had at first followed him in his arrangement of facts, was subsequently constrained to quit his guidance and enter upon a new path. Sulpicius Severus, moreover, is so brief in his record of the events and circumstances connected with the life of Athanasius, that he fails to place anything clearly before our minds, and what he has written is too confused and intricate to be of any real use to the biographer or the historian.

The author of the life of Pachomius is deserving of our commendation, as supplying very many new and interesting facts connected with Athanasius.

Socrates, who—after having, as we have said, followed Rufinus in the earlier books of his ecclesiastical history—was subsequently compelled to abandon his guidance and depend upon himself, derived much of his information from somewhat questionable sources, and his chronology is often involved in no little confusion.

The history of Sozomen is to be preferred to that of Socrates, although it has often been supposed that he obtained most of his details from Socrates. But, in fact, although following the same order of events as Socrates, he has introduced many circumstances illustrative of the life of Athanasius, which Socrates had either passed over or inaccurately described, as, for example, the events which took place at Tyre, and those connected with the expulsion of George from Alexandria, in the year 356 A.D.

Theodoret, although brief and confused in his narrative, is very useful to the biographer of Athanasius from introducing into his history many acts and monuments which are not to be found elsewhere.

Gelasius of Cyzicus can only be followed with the greatest caution; but still we are indebted to him for some genuine letters.

The Greek Lives of Athanasius are for the most part of little value. One of them is the work of an anonymous author, who derived most of his facts from the writings of Socrates, Sozomen, and Theodoret, adding the names of prefects not found elsewhere, and many mythical stories, which detract from his credit as a historian, and can only be received with much caution.

The Life in the "Library of Photius" abounds with trifles; that which is named the "Vita ex Metaphraste" is somewhat preferable, but is composed of scraps sewn together, and borrowed from various sources; and the Life translated from the Arabic by Renaudot, and communicated by him to Montfaucon, is full of glaring follies and absurdities, congenial to the Coptic mind.

Such is the estimate formed of some of the chief biographies of Athanasius by Montfaucon in the preface to his admirable Life in Latin prefixed to the

Benedictine edition of Athanasius's works.

Of the birth, parentage, and boyhood of this great champion of the truth, we know either nothing at all, or the information we possess is most scanty. Far more is recorded, either by themselves or by others, of the early days of Augustine and Chrysostom, than is handed down to us of the childhood of Athanasius.

We find a confirmation—if that indeed were needed—of his having been born at Alexandria, in a statement made by Constantine in a letter recalling Athanasius from his second exile, in which he alludes to Alexandria as the banished prelate's "native home." This is recorded in Athanasius's "Apology against the Arians" (51). Moreover, not only do the majority of writers relate that Alexandria was the birthplace of Athanasius, but he himself not unfrequently intimates the same fact; and, when in exile, asserts in a letter sent to Lucifer (Ep. 2, "ad Lucif."), that the Arians, watching at the gates and approaches to the city, had, since he had escaped from their hands, debarred him from the power of visiting his parents.

It would seem evident that his father must have lived within a reasonable distance from Alexandria—if not, as is more probable, in Alexandria itself—since the historian Socrates (iv. 13) relates that, when an edict or order from the prefects of the Prætorium disturbed the Church of Alexandria, Athanasius, afraid of the irrational violence of the multitude, and fearing lest he should have to bear the blame of any of the absurd extravagances that might be committed, concealed himself for four whole months in his father's tomb. But when the populace, vexed at his absence, grew tumultuous by reason of their love and affection for him, the Emperor, understanding that on this account

Alexandria was gloomy and sorrowful, signified by
letter that Athanasius should securely and without fear
continue in possession of the churches. And this was the
reason, adds the historian, why the Alexandrian Church
continued undisturbed until the death of Athanasius.

We can scarcely suppose that Athanasius would have
sought safety in his father's tomb if it had been situated
at any distance from the city, since in that case he might
have chosen, without any fear of detection, some more
convenient and satisfactory place of retreat.

We also find mention made of an aunt of his, who,
during the period of his second banishment, suffered
severe persecution and ill-treatment at the hands of the
Arians, who probably directed against her that cruelty
which they would otherwise have shown towards her
nephew, had he been present ("Hist. Ar.," 13; and
"Apol. c. Ar.," 9).

These are, indeed, most meagre details of the family
records and reminiscences of so great and remarkable a
man. We cannot positively tell how he was brought up
at home, or what religious or other influences were at
work all around him. We cannot pretend to say whether
he had the inestimable advantage which Augustine and
Chrysostom and Gregory Nazianzen enjoyed, of having
a devoted mother to watch over his infancy and
childhood, and to screen him from early temptations
and sin.

Alban Butler, indeed, in his "Lives of the Saints,"
writes:—"His parents, who were Christians, and
remarkable for their virtue, were solicitous to procure
him the best education." He does not, however, give any
authority for the assertion. And Cave (p. 38) says:—
"His parents—though the silence of antiquity has
concealed their names—are said to have been peculiarly

eminent for piety and virtue, who left no other child but him, as if Heaven designed him on purpose to be the sole heir both of their estate and virtue." Montfaucon, also, in his Life prefixed to the Benedictine edition of Athanasius's works, agrees for the most part with this estimate formed by the two writers just mentioned.[1]

Nor can we affirm what were the family circumstances in which he was brought up—what was the rank in life which his father held—or what was the social, moral, or intellectual environment that surrounded him. We might infer from the tenor of his own language addressed to Constantine, that his private resources were but scanty.

The exact date of his birth is also involved in no slight a degree of uncertainty. It probably occurred in the year 296 A.D., though some writers have thought that it took place in 290 A.D. Athanasius tells us in his "History of the Arians" (64) that he had no personal recollection of the persecution under Maximian that took place in the year 303 A.D. Had he been born before the year 296—which is usually assigned as the date of his birth—it can scarcely be supposed that he would have retained no remembrance of the cruelties then inflicted upon the Christians. And, moreover, when he was made bishop, soon after 325 A.D. (the time of the Nicene Council), he was regarded as a decidedly young man—too young, in fact, according to the Arians, to have been legally consecrated, though he would then have been, in accordance with the earlier reckoning, in his thirty-seventh year.

Nor, again, can we suppose that he was born subsequently to the year 296 A.D., inasmuch as he tells

---

[1] Montfaucon's words are:—"Parentes ejus pii, Christiani, ac, si qua fides inferioris ævi Scriptoribus, nobilitate et opibus insignes."

us in his treatise on the "Incarnation of Christ" (56), that he received some instruction in divinity from persons who underwent persecution in the year 311 A.D., during the reign of Maximin II.—instruction of which the mind of a mere child would scarcely have been receptive. And, moreover, since it would seem clear that the two first treatises which he composed were written before the year 319 A.D., it would be scarcely possible to conceive that writings equal in learning and power to the works of any of the Fathers could have been composed by one born, as some have conjectured, at the beginning of the century, when he would only have been nineteen years of age.

It cannot, perhaps, be asserted that these are demonstrative evidences as to the date assigned to Athanasius's birth. They may possibly admit of refutation, or at any rate furnish grounds for doubt or discussion on the subject. They have, however, appeared sufficiently strong to so thoughtful and diligent a biographer as Montfaucon, and to so accurate and painstaking a Church historian as Professor Bright, to induce them to place with a feeling of comparative certainty the birth of Athanasius in the year 296 A.D.

One story, and one only, has come down to us respecting the boyhood of Athanasius, and even in regard to this there are some who have viewed it as a "very doubtful," if not an apocryphal narrative. The story is found in Socrates, the Church historian (i. xv.), who informs us that he quotes the greater portion of it from the "History of Rufinus" (i. 14). The tale runs thus:—"Athanasius, when very young, was playing with some companions of the same age as himself a kind of sacred game, which consisted in an imitation, on their part, of the sacerdotal functions and of the clerical order.

In this play Athanasius was elected to fill the office of bishop, while each of the other children acted either as a presbyter or a deacon. This species of sacred game they were playing on the day on which the anniversary of the martyrdom of Peter the bishop, who had suffered in the Diocletian persecution, was being observed. It so happened that Alexander, the bishop of Alexandria, who was about to entertain some of his clergy in a lofty building overlooking the sea beside the harbour, observed the group of children playing on the edge of the shore, and was struck by the serious aspect of their game. Having afterwards sent for all of them, he inquired what place had been allotted to each of them in the game, supposing that from what had been done, something might be prefigured or portended concerning each of them. From what he heard, he gave orders that the children should be brought up in the Church and educated, and, of all of them, more especially Athanasius. These things, Socrates adds, are related by Rufinus in his Ecclesiastical History concerning Athanasius, nor does he think it at all unlikely that these things happened, for many such like acts, he says, have frequently been found to have taken place. Rufinus himself narrates this additional circumstance. He states that the boys, upon Alexander's inquiry, confessed that some Catechumens had been baptized by Athanasius, whom they had, as we have seen, chosen as bishop in their game. Upon Alexander's demanding of those said to have been baptized, what questions they had been asked, and what answers they had returned, and after having examined him who had asked the questions, it was found that all things had been done in strict accordance with the rites of the Church of Christ. After consultation with his clergy, Alexander is said to have ordered that the boys on whom the water had been poured—after they had been duly questioned, and had returned full and sufficient answers—should not be re-baptized.

Such is the story which has been told of the boyhood of Athanasius,—a story of whose verisimilitude Dean Stanley ("Lectures on the Eastern Church," p. 264) has spoken in favourable terms, and as "having every indication of truth,"—and which has been fairly regarded as presignifying the position which Athanasius was destined afterwards to fill in the Church of Christ. It indicates at least one circumstance which is worthy of notice, and which has a close reference to his character at that early period of his life. It points out Athanasius as holding by the conviction and choice of his equals in age, either an intellectual or a moral superiority, when compared with themselves, and as thus evincing even in his tender years indications at least of that mental supremacy, resolution of will, determination of character, and mastery and control over other minds, which he so conspicuously manifested in his after life. As Wordsworth writes,
The child is father of the man.

But though Rufinus, the historian, quoted by Socrates, lived within fifty years of the time at which this story is stated by him to have occurred, and Socrates himself wrote within one hundred years of the period, and though consequently they might be supposed to have had some definite knowledge of such comparatively recent events, which could scarcely within that short time have passed into the region of uncertainty and myth—yet, nevertheless, there is a strong chronological difficulty which has to be surmounted before the story is pronounced trustworthy.

It is generally believed that Alexander came to the see of Alexandria after the brief episcopate of Achillas, in the year 313 A.D. In that case—if the birth of Athanasius has been rightly fixed at 296 A.D.—the boy-bishop of the sacred game must have been at least seventeen years old, and came forward as a theological writer before the year 319 A.D. Nor was Alexander a man who would have sanctioned or tolerated such a game in the case of one who had almost reached his eighteenth year. The story is, of course, based upon the assumption that he was much younger than seventeen when he was thus engaged in "enacting holy rites."

It is, nevertheless, difficult to believe that there is not some germ of reality, even if not "every indication of truth," in so circumstantial a narrative, which approved itself to two such writers as Rufinus and Socrates, who lived so close to the time at which it was said to have taken place.

However pleased persons may have been to trace out indications of future greatness in the boyhood of so distinguished a man, and however much Alexander may have been disposed to credit the youthful promise of his great successor, it can scarcely be imagined that so minute, circumstantial, and definite a story could have been concocted so shortly after the supposed time of its occurrence, or have gained the credence of two such conscientious Church historians living so close to the time recorded in the narrative, if it were a pure myth or fable (as Cave suspected it to be)—a mere legend in which no real belief could be placed.[2]

---

[2] Alban Butler speaks of Alexander "*before* he was raised to the episcopal chair" of Alexandria, being "much delighted with the virtuous deportment of the youth (Athanasius), and with the pregnancy of his wit."

CHAPTER III
Athanasius Appointed Secretary to Alexander

But whether we deem it right to give credence to the tale just told or not, it is clear from the testimony of Sozomen (ii. 17), that Alexander received the youthful Athanasius into his house, convinced in his own mind of the distinguished future which was in store for him, and having formed the highest opinion of his fitness for the clerical calling. He, moreover, employed his services as a secretary. Such a position was most favourable to the mental and moral training of Athanasius. To be received as an inmate into the episcopal palace at Alexandria, and thus to become intimately associated with one who occupied the "evangelical throne," and stood second among the prelates of the Christian Church, was indeed a high honour for the youthful Athanasius Such intercourse and such companionship could not have failed to produce their fruits in his life and character. He would thus be able to gain complete information of all that was being carried on in that important and extensive diocese which claimed St. Mark as its first bishop. He was brought into close contact with one, who, as Patriarch of Alexandria, and as Archbishop and Metropolitan, occupied nearly the highest position in the Christian Church, and was distinguished by the title of "Papa" or Pope. Alexander exercised authority over nearly one hundred bishops,—all the Churches throughout Egypt, the Pentapolis, and Libya being subject to his jurisdiction. It was almost a royal sovereignty that the prelate of Alexandria claimed; and, consequently, one who was brought, like Athanasius, under his immediate influence, and admitted into private and personal intimacy with him, not only gained indirectly a position of the highest importance, but also had an opportunity of acquiring a wide experience and ample knowledge of affairs, and of meeting with all sorts and conditions of men, from the very highest rank downwards. To be on such familiar terms with the patriarch, that the relation could be viewed respectively as "fatherly" on the one side and "filial" on the other, was an honour few could hope to enjoy. And the pleasure of this companionship must have been increased by the well-known kindliness and courtesy of the bishop—a man "quiet and gentle," as Rufinus tells us (i. 1), and attractive in manners and bearing, though able to act, when circumstances required it, with spirit, decision, and vigour. All this must have told greatly upon Athanasius in the formation of his character, the enlargement of his mind, and in broadening the sympathies of his nature.

We have already hinted that it was impossible for a man of keen intelligence, natural talents, and quick perception, to have lived in such a city as Alexandria—so full of scientific thought, of commercial activity, and religious speculation, and of men of various nationalities—without having his intellect strengthened,

his knowledge of men and things enlarged, his logical
and dialectical powers sharpened and refined, and his
acquaintance with the various theories of philosophers,
and the different modifications of religious views and
theological systems proportionately increased.

His own mind was naturally fitted to grasp and retain
all the diversified questions and problems which were
brought before it. We can form a fair conjecture what
his natural powers and abilities were in his youthful
days by observing what they proved to be when
developed in after life, and when by longer study and
careful training they had become matured and
consolidated.

We have seen how Paganism, Judaism, and
Christianity all grew up side by side in Alexandria; and
how an eclectic philosophy sought to harmonise the
different elements of various religious creeds together,
and to extract from each the points in which they
agreed, and thus to form a system which should
embrace all the fancied excellences of each.

The great temple of Serapis bore witness to the still
existing presence of Paganism; to the belief in the old
Egyptian idolatry; to the worship of Osiris, Isis, Apis,
and the like; and to all the peculiar and deeply-rooted
rites and ceremonies which gave a marked and
distinctive colouring to the worship that still held its
ground in Egypt, even though Grecian philosophy, and
Hellenised Judaism, and the Christian religion were all
endeavouring to drive it from its ancient seat.
Athanasius also might have seen in the "Cæsarium" the
deification of the Cæsars, and hence gained an insight
into the religion of ancient Rome. Moreover, in the
great libraries of the city he could have learned much in
connexion with the worship of an elder Paganism, and

marked its hold upon the nations gradually relaxing, as
well as its incapability of satisfying the cravings of the
heart of man.

With so large a mass of Jews on every side residing in
the city, his active and thoughtful mind would have
desired to understand the prominent features of their
religion, toned down and softened as it was by the
mixture of foreign elements—by the allegorising
tendencies of the school of Philo, and by the
disintegrating tendencies of an eclectic philosophy. He
might still have seen instances of what it was in its
simpler and more rigid past, as well as what it had now
generally become in the more liberally-minded city of its
adoption.

He would observe the tendency of Neo-Platonism to
widen, but not to deepen the views of those who
adopted it; to foster in its advocates liberalism and
comprehensiveness, at the expense of simplicity and
tenacity of grasp. He would be able to discover its weak
points, the feebleness of its hold upon the human heart,
its adaptation rather to an exhausted condition of the
human mind which had passed its prime than to the
fresh vigour of an early civilisation, with its firm grasp of
the present and its ardent hopes for the future. He would
be enabled, also, to unravel the fine-drawn and subtle
distinctions and theories of the critical, the grammatical,
and the rhetorical schools in the city; and observe how
refinement and verbal nicety had taken the place of
vigorous thought and the truthful deductions of plain
common-sense; and how literary composition had sunk
into imitation and a feeble copying of a purer and
stronger age of thought, and feeling, and expression.

From quotations that occur in his writings ("Orat."
iv. 29), he would seem to have been familiar with the

poetry of Homer; and acquaintance with the prevailing philosophy must have familiarised him with the views and theories of the illustrious Plato. His mind must have been carefully trained at this period of his life. He must have drunk deeply at the springs of science and logic, as well as of theology, or else he would never have been fitted at so young an age to produce works of no common or ordinary character. From passages that occur in his writings, as, for instance, in his "Treatise against the Gentiles" (40), it is evident that he took pleasure in tracing out the arguments that natural religion advanced for the necessity of a great First Cause and Creator of all things, and for the existence of the soul from the longing after immortality in man.

Whether—in accordance with the opinion of Sulpicius Severus (ii. 36)—he became a student of Roman Law, we can scarcely dare to affirm or deny, though a degree of confirmation is afforded of his having done so by the statement of Socrates (i. 31) that "he took the legal exceptions" to the charges in the Council held at Tyre. Socrates writes: "But in the disproof of the false accusations brought against Macarius, he made use of legal exceptions."

But although we cannot for a moment doubt that Athanasius devoted thoughtful attention to the writings and practices of Paganism, to Jewish ceremonial, and to rabbinical dogmas, yet we are constrained to believe from all he wrote, all he taught, all he did, and all he suffered, that his great interest was centred in the faith of Christianity, and in those sacred writings to which it appealed in proof of its doctrines and its form of belief. We have every reason to infer from his own statements that he, like Augustine and Chrysostom, was not only a diligent student, but a warm and reverent admirer of the

Holy Scriptures. This is proved from various passages scattered throughout his different writings. A biographer of the last century has remarked that "from his easy and ready manner of quoting the Holy Scriptures, one would imagine he knew them by heart; that at least by the assiduous meditation and study of those divine oracles, he had filled his heart with the spirit of the most perfect piety, and his mind with the true science of the profound mysteries which our divine religion contains" ("Lives of the Saints," v. 16).

We can scarcely fail to see that the great object of his earlier life was a preparation for the work in which he was afterwards engaged; that to this end he must have devoted all his energies, and that this was the final goal which he must have set before him. Otherwise, he could never have written as he subsequently wrote; he could never have carried on the grand controversy which is so completely associated with his name, nor could he ever have undergone all the sufferings and trials which he endured in its behalf, through so long a period of time, without relaxing or succumbing in his great and perilous work. Nor was this all; for he had been also called upon to learn the hard and stern lessons which persecution could teach. He had lived through the cruelties inflicted upon Christians by that relentless tyrant Maximin II., and had witnessed the power of faith proving victorious over the merciless edicts of a hard-hearted Pagan. He had seen, with deepest grief of heart, when he had scarcely reached his sixteenth year, the Christian teachers whom he loved and reverenced looking forward day by day to the pains of martyrdom. He had dwelt, too, upon the memory of that good bishop of his Church, Peter the Martyr, who had died in the cause of Christ, witnessing a good confession. Thus had he lived with actual men and women who had sacrificed their lives for the faith, and had learned to form a clear estimate of the courage with which they suffered martyrdom, and had endeavoured to imbibe the noble and fearless spirit in which they had fought the good fight. And so it was, that when the time came for him to undergo danger, and peril, and exile in his Master's service, he had, as it were, already rehearsed his part. He could call to remembrance the bearing and the spirit in which many who had gone before him had unshrinkingly endured worse sufferings than those he was called upon to bear, and he had taken well to heart the lesson which their brave and undaunted conduct in the cause of Christ so forcibly inculcated. He was thus hardened, as a good soldier, for his after-life, and rendered proof against the sarcasm and the ridicule which an unfeeling Paganism levelled against the professors of the Christian faith.

Nor is it improbable that his spirit was strung to higher deeds by dwelling on the conduct and character of Antony the monk, whose life produced so great an effect upon the famous Augustine. Not only had Athanasius seen and visited Antony in the desert, perhaps about the year 315 A.D., staying with him and serving him as a disciple, and regarding it an honour to pour water on his hands when he washed them (Athan. "Vit. Anton.," 794); but he also subsequently wrote his life, and so learned to admire that monasticism which possessed such charms for some of the greatest of the Fathers of the Church. The evils which were subsequently displayed in the monastic system were less apparent at its commencement than they were in later times. The earnestness, the zeal, the untiring labour, the ardent self-sacrifice and self-devotion of the hermits, were then brought most prominently into view, and contrasted brightly with the sin, the luxury, and the brutality of the world from which they had emancipated themselves. Such an ascetic life had, no doubt, its attractions for the ardent and susceptible temperament of Athanasius. It fired his imagination, and led him to dwell on that saying of Antony to his younger brethren, "that the longest life of spiritual training was nothing to the Ages of Ages and the Crown." "Such were the times" (observes Dean Milner, who was no friend to monasticism, "Ch. Hist.," ii. xi.), "and in public life the abuses of Christianity were so many, that I wonder not that the most godly had the strongest relish for monasticism in an age when the knowledge of the genius of the Gospel was so much darkened."

CHAPTER IV
Earlier Writings of Athanasius

It is probable that about this time, not certainly later
than the close of the year 318 A.D., Athanasius
published his first literary work. We have already
noticed how his mind had been employed for some
years past, and with what diligence he must have
devoted himself to study and reflection: for on no other
supposition can the peculiar condition of his mind in his
after life, and the nature of the work which he
performed, be either accounted for or understood.
Theology is not a science that can be acquired by
intuition, nor can its truths be grasped all at once.
Previous study and an educational training must be pre-
supposed. Hence, though he was still quite a young
man, we are not at all surprised to find that he brought
out two treatises, which, in fact, form one work: an
essay "Against the Gentiles."[3] and an essay "On the
Incarnation of the Word."

These treatises were, doubtless, the outcome of the
thoughts which had been for a considerable time

---

[3] There is another tract written probably about the year 364 a.d., with nearly
the same title, the genuineness of which has been disputed.

working in his mind. They both of them treated of subjects which must necessarily have employed and exercised his intellect, and on which he was likely to have heard much discussion. They were not, it should be remarked, on the subject of the Arian controversy, and were not directly occasioned by it, for that controversy did not spring up into activity until the following year. Allusions to the nature and spirit of that discussion may, no doubt, be detected in these two treatises, but they were clearly not based on the question, nor did they owe their origin to it; and yet they may fairly be regarded as the best possible introduction to the study of the various questions involved in the Arian controversy. They were the product rather of the thoughts and speculations which were agitating the minds of thinking men at that time, and in that place, and naturally flowed out of the line of study and reflection to which his own mind had been directed.

We can trace in his treatise, "On the Incarnation of the Word," an attempt which was then novel—though it was the natural result of the tone of mind and the philosophic theories that prevailed in Alexandria—an attempt to put forward the subject of Christianity in general, and of the Incarnation of Christ in particular, in a *scientific* form before his readers. This was, indeed, a new mode of handling religious truth. As yet theological writings had not assumed that shape in the Church. The work was evidently written for the instruction of one who was a convert from heathenism to the faith of Christianity.

1. In his "Treatise against the Gentiles" we cannot but observe his wide and general knowledge of the truths of Christianity, unaffected and uninfluenced by the more confined and special tone of thought which

runs through his different works on the Arian
controversy. He traces up idolatry to its origin in the
actual corruption of the heart of man; he exhibits, in
fact, its source, its progress, and also its folly. He
displays in this treatise a vast amount of human learning
and culture, and strives to lift men up to a knowledge of
the one true God, not only from the feelings which exist
in the soul of man, but also from a consideration of all
that meets their eye in the material universe around
them. In consequence of the natural corruption of the
heart, man cannot of himself raise the tone of his
affections and of his mind to things heavenly and
spiritual, but his natural tendency is to devote himself to
what is gratifying to his senses and to the lower nature
and element within him. But though this inclination to
evil exists within, and manifests itself in innumerable
ways, he will not allow that man, as a free agent, and as
possessed of free-will, ought to yield to it.

2. His "Treatise on the Incarnation of the Word,"
alike important and deeply interesting, is a sequel to his
"Treatise against the Gentiles." In this treatise
Athanasius in the first place refers to God as the Creator
of all things, since by this means he thinks we shall be
enabled to perceive more clearly the harmony existing
between the scheme of redemption and creation. He
then refutes the Epicurean idea that all things are the
result of chance, by showing that design and order are
clearly traceable in the works of Creation; and also the
theory of Plato, that all things were made of pre-existing
and uncreated matter; and the opinion of those heretics
who had the blindness to assert that God the Creator
was not the Father of our Lord Jesus Christ.

Having thus refuted error, Athanasius goes on to
establish the truth. He shows that God, by our Lord

Jesus Christ, His proper Word, made all things out of nothing; but perceiving that the human race, from the very condition of their nature, could not continue for ever, He did not create men in the same way as He had done the irrational animals, but created them after His own image, and made them participators of the virtue of His own Word, so that having some shadows of the Word, and being made rational, they might continue in happiness, and live the life of the true saints in paradise. Man, however, transgressed the law, and so became subject to the condemnation of death, and when he had thus fallen, he grew more corrupt, until the whole world was filled with wickedness; and so man, created in God's image, fell, and God's work was destroyed. But it seemed to derogate from God's goodness that rational beings, who had once partaken of His Word, should be thus reduced to corruption and non-existence. Death, therefore, could not be allowed to have dominion over man. How, then, could the truth and the power of God be alike maintained? Repentance on man's part could not suffice. The Word of God—the Creator of all things—could alone renew all things, and by suffering for all, intercede with the Father. And so the incorporeal, incorruptible, and immaterial Word of God condescended to come down to this our world, took to Himself a body, like our body, but sinless, and delivered it up to death in the place of us all, and offered it to the Father in loving kindness to us all, that so, as all died in Him, the law of corruption might be obliterated, and He might thus turn again to incorruption those who had turned to corruption. But man's corruption could not be obliterated, unless all men died. The Son of God, as being immortal, could not die. He therefore took to Himself a mortal body, that thus His body might be a sufficient satisfaction for all, though He Himself remained incorruptible, and that thus corruption in the case of man might cease from the gift of the resurrection.

Jesus Christ could alone renew God's image in fallen man, and regenerate the soul. He alone could effectually teach men, and bring them, through Him, to a knowledge of the Father. And thus the Word humbled Himself to appear in the body, that so He might, as Man, draw men to Himself, and persuade them by what He did, that He was not a mere man, but God, and the Word of the true God. He was not contained by anything, but Himself held all things together. He was not bound to the body, but kept it under His dominion. He shows that none but the Saviour—who in the beginning made all things out of things that were not— could make that which is corruptible, incorruptible; that no one but the Image of the Father could renew men after that Image; that no one but the very Life could make immortal that which was mortal; and that no one but the Only-begotten Son of the Father could fully instruct men respecting the Father. Moreover, He alone could rescue men from the sentence of death, by paying the penalty which was their due. His body, indeed, was of the same essence as all human bodies, and, as being mortal, would have died like them; but by the addition to it of the Word, it was consequently placed out of the power of corruption. Objections—to which he replies— have been made to this doctrine; as, for example, that Christ might have died privately, and in the ordinary course of nature, and not have submitted to the disgrace of the Cross; or that, by concealment of Himself, He might have escaped the malice of the Jews.

The Jews might have learned from a study of their

own Scriptures that Jesus was the promised Messiah. In Him alone were the different predictions of their prophets fulfilled. And, turning to the Gentiles, Athanasius showed that it was fitting that the Word should have taken up His abode in man, rather than in any of the more beautiful parts of the universe, because man needed both teaching and salvation; and that it was necessary that life should be attached to the body in the place of corruption, and that the body could not have put on immortality, unless the Word had assumed it.

Athanasius, moreover, appealed to the effects which Christianity has wrought, in order to show that it was the Divine Word who came down to the earth to proclaim it; such effects as the conversion of the Gentile world, their renunciation of heathenism, and the mighty change effected in the lives of Christian converts. Thus the Word was made man, in order that we might be deified. He manifested Himself through the body, in order that we might attain the idea of the invisible Father.

He concludes the treatise by exhorting us to study with care the Inspired Scriptures, wherein we learn that He who once came in humility shall hereafter return in glory, no longer to suffer on the cross, but to bestow on all men, as the outcome of His crucifixion, incorruption and immortality; no longer to be judged, but Himself to be the Judge of all men—to reward the righteous, and to punish the guilty.

From this analysis of the work we can see that Athanasius, true to his faith, refers everything to the person of Christ, who is brought forward with clear and decisive prominence as the Redeemer and the God-man; as the Head and Representative of mankind; as the Image and Brightness of the Father; as Co-eternal and

Co-equal with the Father; as the Spotless Victim and the Vicarious Sacrifice for man; as the Resurrection and the Life; as the Conqueror of death, and the Creator and Lord of all creation. He speaks also of the fitness there is that He, who is the Wisdom of the Everlasting Father, should be the great Teacher of man, and the Revealer of the will of God.

On all these different points the language of Athanasius is scriptural and orthodox. He does not profess, in a work of this nature, to make a direct personal application to the conscience of his readers of the great truths to which he had directed their attention. This would have been outside and apart from the guiding principle with which the work was written. He was composing a theological treatise, but not applying the truths taught, as he would have done in a sermon or homily. The application to the conscience was naturally and necessarily indirect.

We may remark that, even at this early stage of his literary career, his style of writing was grave, logical, argumentative and clear, full of vigour and energy. His earliest writings bear undeniable testimony to his strong sense, as well as to his firm grasp of the subject which he is handling; and the language in which his thoughts are expressed is terse, nervous, and persuasive,—the true exponent, in fact, of the ideas that filled his mind. It is not a style which appeals to the feelings and imagination, as Chrysostom's did. It addresses itself rather to the reason and the intellect. It is full of acuteness, and even subtlety: it is logical rather than metaphysical; it is always masculine, sometimes even dictatorial and imperious; it never descends to the quibbles and refinements of the scholastic writers, nor is it bound by the mere terminology of logic and the rhetorical art; it always exhibits the writer as firmly convinced and assured of the undoubted certainty of the truths which he advocates, and as incapable of being driven away from the position which he has taken up; it presupposes the truth and the authority of Christianity, and makes no allowance, or very little, for the doubts or difficulties of his opponents.

In confirmation of his argument he does not hesitate to make frequent appeals to Holy Scripture, especially when the points under discussion are closely connected with the subject of revelation.

It is the opinion of Erasmus that Athanasius was not harsh and rugged like Tertullian, or affected like Jerome, or laboured like Hilary, or full of redundancies like Augustine and Chrysostom, or devoted to elaborate composition like Gregory Nazianzen, but wholly absorbed by the matter in which he was engaged, and intent upon the argument before him. Thus, too, Abbot Cosmas is said to have remarked, "When thou meetest with any tract of Athanasius, and hast no paper at hand on which to transcribe it, rather than fail, write it upon thy coat" (Cave, 193).

It is the observation of Photius (Cod. 140) that the "diction and style of St. Athanasius is clear, majestic, full of deep sense, strength, and solid reasoning, without anything redundant or superfluous. He seems to hold the next place in eloquence after St. Basil, St. Gregory Nazianzen, and St. Chrysostom."

Dean Milman has said ("Hist. Christ.," iii. 5) that "in the writings of Athanasius is embodied the perfection of Polemic divinity."

Athanasius's works may be classified under the heads of Polemical, Doctrinal, and Historical. The first are directed either against heathens or heretics; the second

are occupied with stating and explaining the chief
Christian doctrines and verities of the faith; the third
contain the clearest statement of the events and
occurrences of the age in which he lived that is to be
found. All other accounts seem merely borrowed from
him, and diluted in the transfer.

We may add that it was at this time that Athanasius
was appointed a deacon in the Church of Alexandria.
We can readily understand that two such treatises as
those which he had just written could not fail to have
raised him high in the estimation of the bishop, the
clergy, and the more educated of the laity. They must at
once have felt that one possessed of such abilities and
such theological learning ought not to be lost to the
Church. Everything, therefore, seemed to point to his
admission to the Diaconate; and, accordingly,
Alexander, "one whom" (says Cave, 42), "for his piety,
justice, candour, and courtesy, kindness to all, and
charity to the poor, both clergy and people had in great
veneration," not only admitted him to that sacred office,
but would appear also very shortly to have made him
chief of the staff of deacons—the archdeacon, so to
speak.

Hence he was thrown into still closer contact with the
bishop. All that he did would be done under the bishop's
eye. There can be no doubt, from Alexander's bearing
towards him, that a very close intimacy existed between
the bishop and his young deacon, who had now for
several years been living in his palace, constantly
attending upon him in his office as secretary, and been
known to, and valued by him, from his early youth. We
cannot, therefore, hesitate to believe that a feeling of
loyal attachment and respect bound Athanasius to

Alexander, an attachment which was equally felt by the bishop for his young deacon.

CHAPTER V
Arius the Heresiarch

It was about this period, 319 A.D., that the great opponent of Athanasius came forward into public notice in the Church of Alexandria. Arius was at this time a parish priest at Alexandria, having the charge of a church called Baukalis, one of the oldest and most important of the churches there, containing the tomb of St. Mark. It was situated (according to Neale, "Hist. Alex." i. 116) "in the head of the mercantile part of the city," close to the sea-shore, on a spot of ground which probably derived its name (Boucalia) from the pasturage of cattle. Arius was now well advanced in life, having been born (say some writers) in the year 256 A.D.; whether in Libya—a "country" (it has been quaintly remarked) "fruitful in monstrous and unnatural productions"—or whether, according to Photius and some others, in Alexandria, is a moot-point, though perhaps the weight of evidence is in favour of the former of the two places. Arius had originally been an adherent of Meletius, Bishop of Lycopolis, who had laid great stress on purity of Church discipline, though even to the present day his precise views, and the extent of his deviation from the orthodox standard of belief, remain problematical. Arius, returning to the unity of the Church, was ordained deacon by Bishop Peter, but subsequently excommunicated. Peter, it is said, refused to take off the ban laid upon him, having a presentiment that Arius would cause a schism in the Church, and, according to the "Acts of his Martyrdom," having been expressly forbidden to do so by a vision from heaven; but his successor in the bishopric, Achillas, with greater leniency and indulgence, admitted him again into communion, and gave him the influential position of parish priest of the important church of Baukalis.

Arius is described as a man of ability, trained under Lucian of Antioch, of popular gifts and talents, standing high in the favour of Constantia, widow of Licinius, and Constantine's favourite sister. He was a subtle disputant—a man of daring versatility—proud, factious, restless, and exasperated by opposition. In his appearance there was a great show of mortification; he seemed altogether half-dead as he walked along. Rufinus (i. 1) says of him that he was "religious in semblance and appearance, rather than in reality and truth." He was regarded, however, of sufficient importance to have been nearly elected to fill the "evangelical throne" on the death of Achillas. He might, therefore, have looked upon Alexander with some feelings of bitterness (Theodoret, i. 2), as being the successful competitor for the position for which he himself had been marked out by many, though Philostorgius, the Arian historian ("Church History," i. 3), says that he modestly gave Alexander the precedence at the election, and transferred his votes to him. His tone of mind—which was devoid of all reverential feeling— induced him to carry out to their extreme logical conclusions the views which he had adopted. The opinions he advocated have been thus concisely described by Professor Bright:—"The Son of God could not be co-eternal with His Father. He must, therefore, have come into existence at a very remote period, by the creative fiat of the Father, so that it might be truly said of Him that 'once He was not'; He, therefore, must be regarded as external to the divine essence, and only a creature, although of all creatures the most ancient and august." Such was the nature of the teaching of Arius, who, educated in the dialectics of Alexandria, thought that everything, however mysterious and sacred, could be comprehended by a logical syllogism. He began by regarding the Sonship of Christ as a verity, but concluded by wholly separating His essence from that of the Father. Thus the subject of Arianism involved not merely the question of the Divinity of Christ, and of His real relation to the Father, but the whole doctrine of the Trinity.

Alexander, when he heard that such heretical views were being propagated throughout the city, endeavoured to repress the evil by inviting Arius to an interview. The attempt, however, was made in vain. Arius, with even greater boldness of statement, continued to spread his views. The private interview having thus proved of no avail, the bishop summoned a meeting of the clergy. He allowed free discussion on the subject, and endeavoured to hold the balance with so even a hand, that he was (so Sozomen tells us, i. 15) actually charged with indecision and irresolution—a vacillation which we learn induced a priest named Colluthus to quit the orthodox community, set up a sect of his own, and even venture himself to ordain ministers. But it has been urged in

Alexander's behalf,[4] that the points raised by Arius were novel in themselves, and lay outside the reach of human comprehension,—points upon which a man, conscious of his own fallibility, might well pause before he pronounced an authoritative decision. When, however, after a time, Alexander spoke out boldly, and asserted his belief in the co-equality and eternity of the Son, and insisted on the Unity in the Trinity, Arius ventured freely to criticise his language, which he characterised as inclining towards Sabellianism, or the confusion of Persons in the Godhead (Soc., i. 5), a doctrine which, as we learn from Theodoret (i. 5), was very distasteful to the Alexandrian Church.

The evil still continuing to spread—bishops (according to the description of Eusebius, "Vit. Const.," ii. 61) being engaged in a warfare of words with bishops, the people being split up into different factions, and the heathen, taking advantage of the folly and madness of the Christians, making the most solemn mysteries of the faith subjects of profane ridicule in the theatre— Alexander wrote to Arius and his followers, urging them to renounce their impious views, and this letter was signed by the greater part of the Alexandrian clergy. In this call upon Arius to retract, we find that the youthful Athanasius earnestly joined with the bishop, and that, when Arius was subsequently deposed from his clerical position, the archdeacon acted also in full accord with his diocesan.

It is an unfair assertion on the part of the opponents of Athanasius to say that he acted merely out of respect and filial duty towards his bishop when he joined with him in calling upon Arius to retract, and in his subsequent deposition. Athanasius was a man of far too

---

[4] See Bishop Kaye's "Council of Nicæa," p. 4.

independent a character to act against his conscience, even when loyalty to his bishop urged him in the direction of complaisance. We see no traces of such a subservient spirit in any action throughout his life, either before or after this event. Nor could he be supposed to have acted from the love of controversy and the instinct of theological partisanship; for, at this period, there could have been but little feeling of the kind on this subject in existence. No one who has really studied his character can hesitate to believe that Athanasius saw from the very first, as it were by intuition, the great question that was at stake—the blow that Arianism would deal at Christ as the Redeemer of man. No unprejudiced mind would doubt that Athanasius in this, his first controversy with Arius, was actuated by the highest and purest motives, and that he opposed his views because he clearly saw that they militated against the divinity of Christ, and all that Holy Scripture taught on this vital and fundamental point.

Socrates tells us (i. 5), that the first impulse to the controversy was given by Alexander's insisting, at a meeting of the clergy, on the eternity of the Son, to which Arius made an open opposition. The chronological order of events differs slightly in Sozomen's account of the transactions; on the whole, however, the narrative of the latter is fuller, and perhaps more satisfactory.

From an epistle of Arius himself, addressed to Eusebius of Nicomedia, and preserved by Theodoret (i. 5), we gain his own views on Arianism. In that epistle he states, that the Bishop of Alexandria wished to expel him and his followers from that city as Atheists, because we agree not with him when asserting publicly,—"Always God, always the Son"; "At the same time the

Father, at the same time the Son"; "The Son co-exists with the Unbegotten Father"; "The Father does not precede the Son in thought, not for a moment"; "Always God, always Son"; "The Son is from God Himself." … What do we ourselves say? What are our opinions? What have we taught, and what do we teach? This:—"That the Son is not unbegotten, nor a part of the Unbegotten, by any means, nor of any subject-matter; but that by will and counsel He existed before the times and the ages, perfect God, the only begotten and unchangeable; and before He was begotten, or created, or defined, or founded, He was not, for He was not unbegotten. We are persecuted because we say, "The Son hath a beginning," but "God is without beginning." For this we are persecuted; and because we say, that "The Son is from non-existence, or from things that had no previous existence"; which assertion we make, because He is no part of God, nor from any pre-existing substance. For these reasons they trouble us. Thou knowest the rest. (Cf. Wordsworth's "Church History," i. 437; and Milner's "Church History," ii. iv.)

Another statement of Arius's views is this:—"That God was not always a Father, but there was a time when He was only God, and was not yet a Father; that afterwards He became a Father, and that the Son was not always such.… That there is a Trinity, but not all alike in majesty, whose subsistencies are unmingled with one another, one being more immensely glorious than another, and that the Father, as being without beginning, is as to His essence different from the Son: that, in short, the Father is invisible, ineffable, incomprehensible to the Son; and that it is evident that that which has a beginning, can never thoroughly understand or comprehend the nature and quality of that which is without a beginning; that there are three subsistencies, and that God, as being the cause of all, is alone without beginning; that the Son was begotten of the Father without time, and made and settled before time, but was not before He was begotten, and as such did alone subsist with the Father; that He is not eternal, nor co-eternal, nor begotten together with the Father, nor has the same being with Him, as some affirm, introducing two unbegotten principles."

Hence Arius asserted that God was, before He was a Father; that He was before the Son, not only in order of nature, but of time; that the Son, though begotten of Him, has not the same essence, power, and glory with Him; not made of His substance, or at all partaking of His nature, or existing in His essence, but altogether different both in nature and power, though formed to the perfect likeness of it. Whence, then, did Arius derive these views? It has appeared probable to some that he derived them from the doctrine of the later Platonists, who, at that time, governed the schools at Alexandria; or, according to others, from the teaching Aristotle.

The bishop, however, was not satisfied with imposing by himself alone a sentence of deposition on Arius. He, therefore, in the year 321 A.D., convened a provincial synod of one hundred of his suffragan bishops, who were gathered together at Alexandria from Egypt, the Pentapolis, and Libya (Soc., i. 6). Arius and his followers—who consisted of two bishops. five priests, and six deacons—were called upon to state their views categorically before the assembly. It was then ascertained that in Arius's view—to use the words of Canon Bright ("History of the Church," 13),—"The Son of God was the first of creatures, and in that sense the only-begotten; created after the image of the Divine

Wisdom, and therefore called the Word; created in order that by His means God might create us; incapable of thoroughly knowing either the Father's nature or His own. One awful question remained. The Arians were asked whether this exalted creature could change from good to evil? They answered, 'Yes, He can.' "

After this terrible statement their views were pronounced heretical by the members of the council, and he and his followers were excommunicated for their denial of the divinity of the Son, and a solemn anathema pronounced against them.

But this spirit of rationalistic thought—for such was the tone of Arianism—was not checked even by the excommunication of Arius and his party (Theodoret, i. 2). The views advocated by them even grew more popular. They spread widely throughout Alexandria and the Mareotis, among women as well as among men. There was a certain attraction about them to persons who disliked definite dogma—who had any partiality for the views advocated by some of the older heretics— who desired to be freed from the more rigid discipline of the Church, and to embrace a more elastic form of doctrine, or who wished to possess some safeguard, as they thought, against the more materialistic aspect of Sabellianism. There was, consequently, as Bishop Wordsworth has remarked, much that was specious and alluring in Arianism. It studiously shunned an approach to the bolder heretical dogmas, which had shocked the faith of Christendom. It claimed to be a safeguard of Monotheism against Paganism. It condemned Pantheism. It professed reverence for Holy Scripture. It claimed also the merit—no slight one in a learned city like Alexandria—of conciliating Greek philosophy, and of attracting it to Christianity, and of explaining the profoundest mysteries of the faith. It appealed to human reason, and magnified the claims of logic and metaphysics, and proposed to enlist them in the service of religion and the Church. Arius soon discovered that he could not expect to hold his position at Alexandria after being excommunicated by the bishop. He therefore withdrew to Palestine, where he found Eusebius of Cæsarea, and some other bishops in that quarter, willing to listen favourably to his opinions, and even to appeal to Alexander in his behalf.

Arius, moreover, so far from being silenced by the proceedings taken against him, is said to have put forward at this time, with the hope of making his views more popular, a work of an amusing and poetic character, named "Thalia," or the "Banquet," of which book fragments only are extant, which are found in the writings of Athanasius. It was written in a metre which was associated with heathen poetry of a dissolute character—the Sotadic verses—which were notorious, even amongst the heathen, for their grossness. In this poem a scoffing irreverence is displayed; and all the holiest conceptions of the Son of God are flippantly denied, in a style and language likely to catch the fancy of the lower classes of society and to pander to the tastes of the profane. It is also said that Arius composed hymns, which were to be sung by sailors, or travellers, or workmen at the mills, expressing his religious views. It is the opinion of Neander (iv. 32) that in the songs above mentioned there was nothing really poetical, except the mere form in which they were composed.

In answer to the appeal of Eusebius of Cæsarea in favour of Arius, Alexander wrote a letter which he must have addressed to other members of the episcopate as well, since Epiphanius asserts that seventy such letters were preserved in his day, urging them all not to be deceived by the subtlety of Arius. Moreover, in his encyclical letter, Alexander characterised the Arians as transgressors of the law, and authors of an apostasy which might fairly be called the "forerunner of Antichrist"—a phrase which is not unfrequently applied to Arianism by Athanasius. We learn from this letter not only the views which Arius held, but also the method of refutation from holy scripture which Alexander adopted, and the reasons why the synod at Alexandria had excommunicated Arius. This encyclical letter was signed by the clergy of his See, one of them being Athanasius.

In a letter which Alexander wrote to his namesake, the Bishop of Constantinople, which is given in Theodoret (i. 4), he inveighed against the Arians for their Pagan and Judaic view of Christ, for their persecuting tendencies, and their intellectual pride and subtlety. In this somewhat prolix epistle Alexander maintains the doctrine of an Eternal Father and an Eternal Son, whose Sonship is not by adoption, but by essence. Such a view as this, he affirms, neither involves Sabellianism, nor Ditheism, nor any partition of the Divine essence, nor any denial of the Father's prerogative as the Unbegotten.

These letters having proved influential with several of the Palestine bishops, Arius deemed it prudent to repair to Eusebius of Nicomedia, formerly Bishop of Berytus, in Syria, who advocated his cause and wrote to Alexander, praying him to admit Arius again to Church privileges.

Soon, however, the controversy spread over the whole of the Eastern Church. The question also at this time assumed, in one respect, a still greater importance.

Through the personal influence of Eusebius, the crafty
Bishop of Nicomedia, the Emperor himself was induced
to take part in the controversy. He treated the dispute at
first as a mere question of words and terms—a
logomachy or wordy-war—and wrote a letter to
Alexander and to Arius (Soc., i. 7; Euseb., "Vit.
Const.," ii. 62, 64), censuring them for disturbing the
peace of the Church by such a verbal controversy on
trivial and most minute points. Constantine commenced
his letter by saying that, in his administration of the
empire, he had a twofold object before him—one object
was to promote harmony of opinion respecting the
Deity, the other to heal the diseases which he found
existing when he became Emperor. He then expressed
his surprise and grief to learn that even Eastern bishops
were in antagonism on so unimportant a point, which
they had suffered to mar the unity of the Church. Let
them forgive one another, and let each quietly maintain
his own opinion, and not disturb the peace of the
Church. He declared that he had no inclination to be an
eye-witness of such dissensions, and concluded by
entreating them to give him back the peaceful days he
once enjoyed, and his nights free from all anxiety, and
begged them to open out to him a way to the East, by
putting an end to their quarrels, and enable the people to
rejoice and give thanks to God for the restoration of
peace and tranquillity.

The Emperor despatched Hosius of Corduba
(Cordova), the capital of Spain, a distinguished prelate,
to Alexandria to convey the Imperial letter to
Alexander. Hosius, however, was so convinced by his
visit of the importance of the controversy, and that it
could not be quietly set aside as a matter of indifference,
that he induced Constantine to call together a general or

Œcumenical Council of the Church (Euseb., "Vit. Const.," iii. 6, 7), to discuss the whole subject, and to decide the points at issue, in order that peace and unity might be established in the Church and the Empire on this burning question, and also to arrive at a conclusion upon one or two other points respecting which disputes existed in the Church. The two chief points were the question of the Meletian Schism, and the proper time for keeping Easter.

It was necessary that a council should be summoned; for it was now evident that the question of Arianism had become a vital question, affecting all the highest interests of Christianity, and, not only so, but a question which might—as it did, in fact—imperil the very stability of the Roman Empire in the East, keeping both Church and State in a continual excitement for the next hundred years to come. It was by no means—as Constantine first thought it—"a fruitless logomachy, revolving about a Greek iota" ('Homöousios,' 'Homoiousios'), but entered into the very heart of the Christian religion.

The Arian system has been well described as a refined form of Paganism, which substituted a created demigod for the eternal and uncreated Logos. It made a breach between God and man: it rendered Christ's atonement an impossibility: it degraded Christianity, and its natural tendency was downward by an easy incline to Socinianism and Rationalism, ending in the terrible idea that Christ was a mere man. Hence it was evident that the cause of Christianity was closely connected with the triumph of the views maintained by Alexander and Athanasius.

It is easy to say—as some modern writers have affirmed—that "silence and charity would have been the best means of preserving peace on all sides;" but we must recollect that such a mode of speaking implies that the controversy was, as Constantine first regarded it, a frivolous and a trivial one. But no sincere Christian could then, or can now, deem it a trifling matter, whether his Saviour and Redeemer be believed to be the Creator of all things or a mere creature. "The Soul"—it has been well said—"is of too great consequence for men to hazard its salvation on they know not what. Silence, therefore, was a vice in this case, in which the contention was based on so fundamental a point, though we cannot but regret how little care was often taken of humility and charity, the exercise of both of which is perfectly consistent with a sincere and earnest zeal for the doctrine of the Trinity."

CHAPTER VI
The Council of Nicæa

A remarkable incident in the life of Athanasius is now brought before us. Constantine, as we have seen, determined to lay the question of Arianism before an Œcumenical council. This council was convened, and Alexander, acting upon a wise and discriminating estimate of the character and abilities of Athanasius, took him as his companion and assistant to this great assembly of the primitive Church. The council was held in the early summer of 325 A.D.;—some say on May 20th, others on June 19th—and it probably lasted about two months, though some writers have supposed that it continued three years and six months, and others even a still longer time, but with no just ground for the supposition.

The council met at Nicæa—the "City of Victory"—in Bithynia, close to the Ascanian Lake, and about twenty miles from Nicomedia. Nicæa—founded by Lysimachus and re-built by Antigonus—is called by Strabo (xii. 565) the Metropolis of Bithynia. It was built four-square, and famed for the elegance and symmetry of its architecture. Here it was that the first, as well as the most important,

of all the general councils met. It was an Eastern
council, and, like the Eastern councils, was held within
a measurable distance from the seat of government. The
learning of the Church at that time, with but slight
exceptions, was Eastern. "The controversies"—says
Dean Stanley, in his "Lectures on the Eastern Church,"
67—"on which the councils turned, all moved in the
sphere of Grecian and Oriental metaphysics. They were
such as no Western mind could have originated." Thus
Nicæa was an Eastern city. Of the 318 bishops (such
was the number according to Athanasius, Hilary,
Jerome, and Rufinus) who subscribed its decrees, only
eight came from the West, and the language in which
the Creed was composed was Greek, which scarcely
admitted of a Latin rendering. The words of the Creed
are even now recited by the Russian Emperor at his
coronation. Its character, then, is strictly Oriental. Its
place in our Liturgy is an abiding memorial of the far-off
East.

Even to the present day—while the decisions of other
Œcumenical councils are well-nigh forgotten—the
decrees of the Council of Nicæa are accepted
throughout the universal Church. For Arianism
penetrated also into the Western Church, and made
itself felt. It was the peculiar form of belief of the Goths
who assailed the Roman empire, of Alaric, the
conqueror of Rome, and of Genseric, who subdued
Africa. It prevailed in the kingdoms established by the
Goths, both in the south of France and in Spain.

Though Arianism was confined to the most abstract
region of abstract thought, and though it referred to the
mysterious relations of the Godhead before ever time
was, yet, strange to say, it roused the feelings of men to
the utmost excitement and fury. "Bishop rose against

bishop" (writes Eusebius, "Vit. Const." iii. 4), "district against district, only to be compared to the Symplegades dashed against each other on a stormy day."

To Nicæa—conveyed and maintained at the public expense—flocked the bishops of the East in eager haste, with the greatest enthusiasm and excitement (Eus. "V. C." iii. 6), each attended by two Presbyters and three slaves.

The number of the bishops present, as we have said, was probably 318, so that the Council is not unfrequently spoken of as "The 318." This was the exact number of followers with which the Patriarch Abraham overcame the vast army of the Gentiles (Gen. 14:14; Soc. iv. 12). A crowd of about two thousand persons must have swept into the town, recalling to the mind of Eusebius ("V. C." iii. 6) the description given in the Acts of the Apostles of the multitudes that were gathered together at Jerusalem on the Day of Pentecost—men out of every nation under heaven; though (he adds), at the Nicene Council there were assembled ministers of religion and guides, not merely proselytes and laymen,—men venerable for their age, their constancy, their learning, their wisdom, gathered from the remotest quarters; men not more widely separated and diversified in sentiments, than in person, race, and residence; making up a variegated garland of the most beautiful and rare flowers, which the Christian world never beheld before, nor shall behold again.[5]

There was, no doubt, a great variety in regard to the intelligence and ability of those present; but (as Canon Robertson has observed, "History of Christian Church,"

---

[5] As to the number present, Eusebius ("Vit. Const.", iii. 8) says 250 bishops; Sozomen (i. 17), 320; Julius ("Apol. c. Ar.," 23 ch.) 300; Constantine more than 300 (Soc. i. 9); Athanasius ("Ad Afr.," ch. ii.) 318.

ii. 1, 289) the object of their meeting was not one which required any high intellectual qualifications. For the more subtle arguments and definitions were not introduced into the controversy until a later time (cf. Möhler, i. 227; Dorner, i. 833), and the Fathers who assembled at Nicæa were not so much called to reason on the grounds of their belief, as to witness to the faith which the Church had held on the disputed subjects.

No doubt they came influenced by various feelings, some of a higher and purer, others of a lower and baser kind. It is quite possible that some may have been induced to attend through vanity, and sycophancy, and fear of giving offence, and dread of the imputation of false and mean motives if they stayed away, through ambition, love of applause, and all the ignoble incitements to action that Dr. Jortin ("Ecclesiastical History," book iii.) has cynically gathered together. His description may perhaps apply to some of those who came, but would be glaringly untrue in regard to a large number of those who were urged to be present by the very highest considerations of duty towards God and towards the Church of Christ.

A general council (as Dean Milman has remarked, "Latin Christianity," i. 156), from its very nature and origination, "is not the cause, but the consequence of religious dissension. It is unnecessary, and could hardly be convoked, but on extraordinary occasions, to settle some questions which have already violently disorganised the peace of Christendom. It is a field of battle (he goes on to say), in which a long train of animosities and hostilities is to come to an issue. Men, therefore, meet with all the excitement, the estrangement, the jealousy, the antipathy, engendered by a fierce and obstinate controversy. They meet to triumph over their adversaries, rather than dispassionately to investigate truth. Each is committed to his opinions, each exasperated by opposition, each supported by a host of intractable followers, each probably with exaggerated notions of the importance of the question, and that importance seems to increase, since it has demanded the decision of a general assembly of Christendom."

Notwithstanding a manifest exaggeration and a decided bias in these statements, we must allow that a certain amount of truth underlies them. But, nevertheless, it would seem probable that such feelings and such passions as are here described, exerted less influence over the council of Nicæa, than over any of the general assemblies of which it was the precursor.

Of the 318 members of the Council, we are told by Philostorgius, the Arian historian, that 22 espoused the cause of Arius, though other writers regard the minority as still less, some fixing it at 17, others at 15, others as low as 13. But of those 318 the first place in rank, though not the first in mental power and energy of character, was accorded to the aged bishop of Alexandria. He was the representative of the most intellectual diocese in the Eastern Church. He alone, of all the bishops, was named "Papa," or "Pope." The "Pope of Rome" was a phrase which had not yet emerged in history; but "Pope. of Alexandria" was a well-known title of dignity.

"But close beside the Pope Alexander"—to employ the graphic language of Dean Stanley, which arrests the ear as vividly as a picture does the eye—"is a small, insignificant young man, of hardly twenty-five years of age, of lively manners and speech, and of bright serene countenance. Though he is but a deacon, the chief deacon, or archdeacon, of Alexander, he has closely riveted the attention of the assembly by the vehemence of his arguments. He is already taking the words out of the bishop's mouth, and briefly acting in reality the part he had before, as a child, acted in name, and that, in a few months, he will be called to act both in name and in reality. His humble rank as a deacon does not allow of his appearance in the conventional pictures of the Council. But his activity and prominence behind the scenes made enemies for him there, who will never leave him through life. Any one who has read his passionate invectives afterwards, may form some notion of what he was when in the thick of his youthful battles. That small, insignificant deacon is the great Athanasius."

Athanasius was, in fact, one of the most prominent members of the Council. Gregory Nazianzen "Orat.," 21) speaks of him as one of the most leading men of those who attended on the bishops, and as doing all that in him lay to stay the moral plague of false doctrine. We learn from ancient sources that, as regarded his personal appearance, Athanasius was inclined to stoop, that his features were aquiline, with auburn hair and beard, and a small mouth. His stature was diminutive, and on that account he excited the ridicule and sarcasm of Julian (Ep. 51). His face is described by Gregory as beautiful, like that of an angel. We can fancy him with eager eyes watching the party of Arius, as they were anxiously discussing together how they might, by means of deceptive and evasive answers, satisfy the orthodox. We hear that he manifested a knowledge of Holy Scripture that amazed both friends and foes; and that his clear reasoning and remarkable power of reply and retort, were the subjects of universal remark.

"Next after the pope and deacon of Alexandria," says
the same writer whom we have very recently quoted,
"we must turn to one of its most important presbyters,
the parish priest, as we should call him, according to the
first beginnings of a parochial system organised at
Alexandria, the incumbent of the parish church at
Baukalis. In appearance he is the very opposite to
Athanasius. He is sixty years of age, very tall and thin,
and apparently unable to support his stature; he has an
odd way of contracting and twisting himself, which his
enemies compared to the wrigglings of a snake (cf.
Epiphan., "Hæres.," xxix. 3). He would be handsome
but for the emaciation and deadly pallor of his face, and
a downcast look, imparted by a weakness of eye-sight.
At times his veins throb and swell, and his limbs
tremble, as if suffering from some violent internal
complaint—the same, perhaps, that will terminate some
day in his sudden and frightful death. There is a wild
look about him, which at first sight is startling. His dress
and demeanour are those of a rigid ascetic. He wears a
long coat with short sleeves, and a scarf of only half size,
such as was the mark of an austere life; and his hair
hangs in a tangled mass over his head. He is usually
silent, but at times breaks out into fierce excitement,
such as will give the impression of madness. Yet, with
all this, there is a sweetness in his voice, and a winning,
earnest manner, which fascinates those who come
across him. Amongst the religious ladies of Alexandria
he is said to have had from the first a following of not
less than seven hundred. This strange, captivating,
moon-struck giant is the heretic Arius—or, as his
adversaries called him, the madman of Ares, or Mars"
(Stanley's Lectures, "E. C.," 116).

These were the chief and most important deputies

from Alexandria; but other and strange characters came from the very heart of Egypt; Coptic hermits, such as Paphnutius and Potammon—their very names derived from old Egyptian gods—men who bore upon their persons the ghastly evidences of persecution. Socrates (i. 11) tells us that the former wrought miracles, and that he was highly regarded by Constantine, who even used to kiss the socket out of which his eye had been forced. There were also Syrian deputies there—the learned and orthodox Eustathius of Antioch; Eusebius of Cæsarea, the son of Pamphilus, the father of ecclesiastical history, but at the same time the friend and confessor of Constantine, whose leanings were to the side of Arius; Macarius, the orthodox bishop of Jerusalem; and Paul of Neo-Cæsarea, whose paralysed hands bore witness to the persecution he had undergone. While from Asia Minor came Leontius of Cæsarea in Cappadocia, claimed by both parties, famed for gifts of prophecy; Eusebius of Nicomedia, a professed defender of Arius, the intimate of the Imperial family and of Constantine himself; Acesius, the Novatian, of ascetic reputation, attended by the boy Auxanon. It was said (cf. Soc. i. 10, 13; and Soz. i. 22), that the Emperor asked Acesius why he was not in communion with the Church, when he agreed with the two decisions of the Council, and that being dissatisfied with his reply, said, "Take a ladder, Acesius, and climb up by yourself into heaven." And James of Nisibis was there, who had lived the life of a wild beast, on mountains and in caverns; and Cæcilian, the famous bishop of Carthage, the early cradle of the Latin Church, the object of the hostility of the Donatists; and Marcellus of Ancyra, one of the strongest and bitterest opponents of Arianism, who seems to have taken the place of Athanasius, if he chanced to be absent from the discussion, though unhappily he was afterwards twice deposed for heresy, and once excommunicated by Athanasius himself; and Spyridion, the strange shepherd—bishop of Cyprus—credited with miraculous powers (Soc., i. 12; Soz., i. 11)—whose remains are still held in reverence at Corfu; and Nicolas of Myra, the foremost figure in the pictures of the Council. There were but few deputies from the Western Church, only eight out of the 318. Of these we may mention Theophilus the Goth—noticeable for his fair complexion—from the far North, the teacher of Ulphilas (Soc., ii. 41), the famous missionary of the Goths; and Hosius of Cordova, whom Eusebius calls the "world-renowned Spaniard," the Emperor's chief councillor in the Latin Church, who had been the bearer of the pacificatory letter—the Eirenicon—from Constantine to Alexander and Arius, who was named (so Athanasius tells us) "the Abrahamic old man, well called Hosius, the 'Holy.' " Sylvester, Bishop of Rome, was too old to attend the Council, and was represented by two of his presbyters, Victor and Vincentius.

Some time was spent in preliminary discussion—often more calculated (says Socrates, i. 8) to amuse than to edify—and in arranging the course of procedure which the Council should adopt. Simple-minded and earnest believers were mixed up with subtle disputants who rejoiced in the strife of words, and free discussion preceded the regular work of the Council. It would, in fact, seem that, previous to the regular business of the Council, some pagan philosophers appeared on the scene, either from a desire to satisfy their curiosity respecting Christianity, or from a wish to involve Christians in a cloud of dialectical subtleties, and so to produce contradictions among them. Strange stories also are told of the way in which learned theologians were baffled by some simple-minded layman, and how a famous heathen philosopher, notorious for his arrogancy and pretension, was foiled by an old priest or bishop (Soc., i. 8; Soz., i. 18; and cf. Milner's "Ch. Hist.," ii. 57).

Faithful to Arius, through good report and through evil, were Theonas, Bishop of Marmarica in the Cyrenaica; Secundus, Bishop of Ptolemais in the Delta; Saras, a presbyter from the Libyan province; Euzoius, a deacon of Egypt; and Achillas, a reader. His cause was also supported by Eusebius of Nicomedia, Maris of Chalcedon, and Theognius of Nicæa.

Before the arrival of the Emperor preliminary proceedings took place in a church at Nicæa (Eus., "V. C.," iii. 7). It has been supposed (says Canon Robertson, ii. 1, 289) by some writers that Eustathius of Antioch was president; by some, that the bishops of Alexandria and Antioch presided by turns; while others have assigned the chief place to Eusebius of Cæsarea. The most general opinion, however, is in favour of Hosius, whose name is first among the subscriptions; but there is no ground for the idea that that office belonged to him in the character of a Roman legate, or that he held that character in any way.

The discussions of the Council were at first private. Arius was introduced and examined. He confessed his heresy with a plainness and freedom from all ambiguity, that caused a thrill of horror and indignation to run through the meeting, and many stopped their ears and refused to listen (Athan. "C. Arian.," Orat. 1). Yet even this outspoken heresy was (in the opinion of the learned author of the "Arians," iii. § 1, 270) "far more respectable than the hypocrisy which was the characteristic of his party, and ultimately was adopted by himself."

The Emperor in person presided over the Council. Longing himself for unanimity and peace, he had been distressed by the letters full of recrimination and mutual complaints of each other, which were showered in upon him on his first arrival in the city.

The Council would appear to have been held in the largest hall of the imperial palace (Soz., i. 19; Theod., i. 6), though Valesius, in his notes on Eusebius's life of Constantine (iii. 10), thinks it highly improbable that so sacred a synod should have been held anywhere else than in a church. Seats for the bishops, and benches for the inferior clergy, were arranged in the hall. On a throne in the centre of the room was placed a copy of the Gospels, indicative of the great final appeal in all controversy, or symbolical of the presence of Christ Himself at their meeting. A small gilt seat was placed at the upper end of the hall for the Emperor.

Amid the silent and spell-bound expectation of the whole assembly, who rose immediately to their feet, the renowned Emperor entered the hall alone, without his usual military escort. To the majority he was personally unknown. Never had they been brought face to face with him before. His noble presence; his lion-like eye; his imperial diadem; his splendid purple robe embroidered with gold and precious stones; his surpassing dignity of bearing, mixed with the evident awe and veneration which might be traced in the faltering step with which he walked up the hall to the low seat prepared for him, the colour rushing to his face, as now for the first time he was about to preside over such an assembly of bishops, many of them confessors and well-nigh martyrs for their faith, not even venturing

to take his seat till a sign of permission on the part of the
bishops had been given him;—all this made him look, as
we are told by Eusebius ("V. C.," iii. 10) he did, like an
angel of God come down from heaven.

It would appear that, when all were seated, Eusebius
rose, and, in a species of blank verse, addressed himself
first to the Emperor, and then to the Almighty, in a
hymn of praise for the victory just gained over Licinius.

When Eusebius had resumed his seat, the Emperor
opened the proceedings in a Latin speech, probably
understood by few who heard him, but which was
subsequently translated by the interpreter into Greek, in
which he earnestly and solemnly urged those present to
concord and unity, in that sweet and gentle voice which
was one of his striking peculiarities. The Emperor
assured them that the internal divisions of the Church
were a source of greater grief to him than any foreign
wars. He besought them, therefore, as his friends, as the
ministers of God, and as good servants of their common
Lord and Master, to remove at once from among them
all causes of strife and of controversy, by their obedience
to the laws of peace. By thus acting, he assured them
they would not only do what was acceptable to the Lord
of all, but also to himself, their fellow-servant.

This appeal to concord and charity was sadly needed.
For the bishops immediately began to bring forward
recriminatory charges against each other (Soz., i. 17;
Theod., i. 11), and such bitterness of spirit was
displayed, that the Emperor found it difficult to allay the
ill-feeling and to mediate between them. But at length,
by persuading some and entreating others, and
commending those who spoke well, he was able to bring
them to some degree of unanimity of opinion. Thus he
strove to soften asperities, and conversed familiarly with

those present in the best Greek he could command. Patiently he listened to the arguments of the different prelates and other speakers, sitting as a public moderator (Eus., "V. C.," iii. 13). He disclaimed all wish or intention to dictate to them, regarding himself only as their fellow-servant.

When it was proposed by the party of Alexander and Athanasius that they should take the baptismal faith received in their different Churches as the true sense of holy Scripture and of apostolic teaching, in regard to the Godhead of Christ, and that they should declare Him to be "of God," "the power of God," the "Image of the Father," and "in Him always,"—employing the language of Scripture—the partisans of Arius, after interchanging signs with one another, expressed themselves willing to receive the terms proposed, employing them in their own peculiar sense. Feeling that such terms were not sufficient to bind the Arians, the orthodox were compelled to make use of a term significative "of one essence with the Father," and so had recourse to "Homöousion" as the only form of speech that expressed unequivocally and unmistakeably the notion of the essential Godhead of the Son—His very and true Sonship, and which was the only expression that the Arians could not evade.

It soon became evident that without some explanatory terms, which clearly pointed out what Scripture had revealed, it was impossible to guard against the subtleties of the Arians. What then could the Trinitarians do? To leave the matter undecided, was (as Milner has shown, ii. 58) to do nothing; to confine themselves merely to Scripture terms, was to suffer the Arians to explain the doctrine in their own way. Hence, to censure the Council for introducing a new term, when

all that was meant by it was to express their
interpretation of the Scriptures, would be most
unreasonable.

Constantine, after delivering his address, ordered the
different recriminatory letters which he had before
received, but which he assured them with a solemn oath
he had not read, to be burned in a brazier before them
all, urging them and exhorting them at the same time to
brotherly love and charity.

A Creed was proposed by Eusebius of Cæsarea—the
Creed which he had learned in his childhood—the
Creed of the Church of Palestine, which the Emperor
and the Arians were willing to receive, but this latter fact
presented a fatal obstacle to its reception by the
orthodox. Though the terms of the Creed were, in the
opinion of the author of the "Arians" (ch. iii. § 1),
orthodox, and would have satisfactorily answered the
purposes of a test if the existing questions had never
been agitated, and were consistent with certain
produceable statements of the anti-Nicene fathers, they
were wholly irrelevant at a time when evasions had been
found for them and triumphantly proclaimed.

The Creed of Eusebius was as follows:—
"We believe in one God, Father Almighty, maker of
all things, visible and invisible, and in one Lord Jesus
Christ, the Word of God, God of God, Light of Light,
Life of Life, the only-begotten Son, the first-begotten of
every creature, begotten of the Father before all ages, by
Whom all things were made; Who for our salvation was
incarnate, and lived among men; Who suffered, and
rose again the third day, and ascended to the Father,
and shall come again in glory to judge both the quick
and the dead. We believe also in one Holy Ghost. Each
of them we believe to be and to subsist—the Father truly

Father, the Son truly Son, the Holy Ghost truly Holy
Ghost; as our Lord when He sent forth His Apostles to
preach, said, 'Go, make disciples of all nations,
baptizing them in the name of the Father, and of the
Son, and of the Holy Ghost.' "[6]

The term "Homöousion,"[7] that is, "Consubstantial,"
"of one substance"—which had sprung into existence
before this time, and which occurred in a letter of
Eusebius of Nicomedia—was appropriated by the
orthodox, acquiesced in by the Emperor, and proposed
as the test of orthodoxy, notwithstanding the complaints
made by the Arian party against it as unscriptural,
materialistic, Montanistic, and Sabellian. It denied—so
they affirmed—the separate existence of the Son; but
from this charge it was successfully vindicated by the
orthodox. It has been observed by Bishop Kaye (Ibid.,
57), that Athanasius himself rarely uses the word in his
statements of the truth. But though the Council adopted
the term "Homöousion," which Luther felicitously
described as a "bulwark of the faith" ("Propugnaculum
fidei"), they refused to give their sanction to the
meaning of, and distinction between, the terms "Ousia"
and "Hypostasis." When the term "Homöousion" was
agreed to by the Council, Hosius and others were
commissioned to draw up a Creed. It was drawn up,
and approved by the Emperor, who now heartily
advocated the side of the orthodox, and regarded the
proposed term as a "divine inspiration."
The Creed proposed was as follows:—

"We believe in one God, the Father Almighty,
Maker of all things visible and invisible; and in one Lord

---

⁶ See Bishop Kaye, "Council of Nicæa," 42, 43.
⁷ On the word "Homöousion," see Newman's "Arians," ch. ii. § 4; and Bull,
"Def. Fid. Nic.," ii. 1.

Jesus Christ, the Son of God, begotten of the Father, only-begotten, that is, of the essence of the Father, God of God, and Light of Light, very God of very God, Begotten, not made, of one essence with ("Homöousion") the Father; by Whom all things were made, both in heaven and in earth. Who for us men and for our salvation came down, and was incarnate, and was made man; suffered, and rose the third day; ascended into the heavens; shall come to judge the quick and the dead. And in the Holy Ghost. But those who say, 'Once He was not;' and, 'Before He was begotten, He was not;' and, 'He came into existence out of nothing;' or, who say, that 'the Son of God is of another substance, or essence, or is created, or mutable or changeable,' are anathematized by the Catholic and Apostolic Church."[8]

According to Socrates (i. 8), all the bishops signed the Confession of Faith except five, viz., Eusebius of Nicomedia, Maris, Theognius, Theonas, and Secundus; but, according to Sozomen (i. 20), seventeen at first were reluctant to subscribe it, though afterwards most of them signed it, being urged (says Philostorgius, i. viii.) by Constantia to do so. The ground of objection taken by them was the employment of the word "Homöousios,"—consubstantial or co-essential. Arius and his extreme followers were banished, and his writings, including his work called "Thalia," were ordered to be burned, his followers being called "Porphyrians" by the Emperor in his edict on the subject. Eusebius of Cæsarea, the Church historian, expressed for some time his doubts respecting the term "Homöousios," and stated in a letter which he wrote on the subject to the members of his Church, that all the

---

[8] Cf. Canon Bright's "Hist.," 24, 25; and Stanley, "E. C.," 163, *seq.*

evil had resulted from the employment of an unscriptural term, and that he had at length been induced to sign for the sake of peace. It is related by their own historian, Philostorgius, that some of the Arian minority sheltered themselves under a palpable deception, when signing the Creed, by the substitution of the term "Hom*oi*ousios" ("of *like* essence") for "Hom*öo*usios" ("of the *same* essence"). This could only be viewed as an unworthy act of duplicity.

After a short time an amnesty was proclaimed, and the followers of Arius were allowed to return; Arius himself being debarred from going to Alexandria. The clemency of the Council of Nicæa was very marked, especially as compared with other and later Councils.

It was evidently supposed that the decisions of the Council of Nicæa would be final, and that an end would thus be put to all theological disputes, at least on this particular subject of controversy. And in this spirit it was that the decrees of Nicæa were formally sanctioned by the Council of Sardica, by the Council of Constantinople in A.D. 381, and still more definitely by the General Council of Ephesus. Nor was the absolute supremacy of the Council of Nicæa at all infringed till the fourth General Council of Chalcedon, when additions to the original Creed were made, and the anathemas abandoned.

It seems strange that in a controversy of so important a character, and at so august and solemn a Council, which has been called "the first real senate of Christendom," we should possess so little definite information respecting the precise arguments employed by either side in the discussion. Thus Gibbon (ch. xxi., note 55) speaks of the transactions of the Council of Nicæa as being related by ancient writers, not only in a partial, but in a very imperfect manner.

Inasmuch as the summoning of the Council of Nicæa was, relatively to the Christian Church, the most important event, next to his conversion, in the life of Constantine, we might have expected to find in the writings of Eusebius, the great historian of the early Church and the eulogist of the Emperor, a complete account of the discussion by which such grave decrees were decided upon. But we look in vain to his History for the information which we naturally desire. Probably, from the result of the Council, he took but little interest in its proceedings, and felt no satisfaction in dwelling upon them. His account is, in fact, most brief and superficial. We have, therefore, to gain our information from the works of Athanasius, and from the writings of three Church historians who lived in the following century—from Socrates, both a native and advocate of Constantinople, named "Scholasticus," whose views were, perhaps, tinctured by Novatianism; from Sozomen, also a layman and advocate of Constantinople, though probably a native of Maiuma, the port of Gaza, in Palestine, whose grandfather was said to have been converted to Christianity by witnessing a miraculous cure performed by the monk Hilarion; and from Theodoret, the Bishop of Cyrus in Syria, who also took part in the Councils of Ephesus and Chalcedon.

We know the conclusion at which the Council arrived; we are in possession of the exact words of the Creed authorised by the Council; and we are acquainted with the famous term "Homöousion," to which a specific meaning was then authoritatively attached. But we are not aware of the different steps and stages in the argument by which the different conclusions were evolved, and the final result attained. We can only speculate upon the arguments which the great champion of the faith, Athanasius, employed in the discussion, and infer from his after-writings what his course of reasoning would probably have been. We might have wished it otherwise; but all that we can now do is to acquiesce in the inevitable. His probable method of argument has been thus briefly drawn out by Professor Bright from a consideration of his subsequent views on this great question which have come down to us in his writings. We may assure ourselves, he thinks, that he would have maintained "that the real Divinity of the Saviour was asserted in many places of Scripture; involved in the notion of his unique Sonship; required by the Divine economy of Redemption; and attested by the immemorial consciousness of the Church."

Though Athanasius himself acknowledges that the members of the Council would have desired to limit themselves to the terminology of Scripture, and though he was himself fully conscious that no expression of human thought could completely and satisfactorily represent the great and mysterious doctrine which was under discussion; still he firmly believed that the term "Homöousion" on which they had fixed, gave, so far as language could give, an adequate and sufficient interpretation of this divine mystery—sufficient to establish the truth and to refute error; and that the result arrived at was not a mere "speculative formula," but an "authenticated symbol" of the claim which the Son of God has upon the love, and reverence, and devotion of man, and that in the clear establishment of such a vital doctrine no labour was superfluous, and no effort too great.[9]

Before the Council dispersed, a synodical letter was addressed to the members of the Church in Egypt, informing them of the manner in which the different questions under discussion had been settled—namely, that Arius had been excommunicated, and his impious opinions condemned; that Meletius was permitted to keep the title of Bishop, but was not allowed to lay hands on any, and that those ordained already by him were to retain their dignity, but be placed after those ordained by Alexander; and that Easter was to be kept, not according to the Jewish calculation, but in accordance with the reckoning which was general throughout Christendom.

In addition to the fore-mentioned decrees made by the Council of Nicæa, it may be briefly stated that twenty authentic canons were also enacted (Theod. i. 8). These canons have been divided into four groups (see Dean Stanley, "E. C." p. 189):—(1) Those which relate to clerical jurisdiction; (2) those which bear upon the morals and manners of the clergy; (3) those referring to cases of conscience; and (4) one, and only one, which related to worship. The apocryphal canons of the Council are said to fill forty volumes. They are, in fact, "a collection of all the customs and canons of the Oriental Church, ascribed to the Nicene Council, as all good English customs are to Alfred."

---

[9] "In speaking of Gibbon's work to me, Carlyle"—says his biographer, J. A. Froude—"made one remark which is worth recording. In earlier years he had spoken contemptuously of the Athanasian controversy, of the Christian world torn to pieces over a diphthong, and he would ring the changes in broad Annandale on the 'Homöousion' and the 'Homœousion.' He told me now that he perceived Christianity itself to have been at stake. If the Arians had won, it would have dwindled away into a legend." ("Life of Carlyle in London," by Froude, ii. 462.)

Before the bishops departed to their different, and in many cases far-distant homes, they were invited by Constantine to a magnificent banquet (it being the solemnity of his "Vicennalia"), which his eulogist Eusebius ("V. C." iii. 15) describes as being a lively representation of the kingdom of Christ, and which was more like a dream than sober reality. He, moreover, distributed presents among them according to their several ranks and merits, and earnestly pressed upon them once more concord, unity, brotherly-kindness, and charity. He also commended himself to the prayers of the bishops.

CHAPTER VII
Athanasius Made Archbishop of Alexandria

The Nicene Council was over, and the character and reputation of Athanasius stood still higher than they had done before in the estimation of the orthodox. His fame must have spread among many who saw and heard him at that Council, to whom before he was almost, if not quite, unknown. Bishops, presbyters, and deacons, from all the remoter quarters of the East, as well as from the distant regions of the extreme West, had learned to appreciate his intellectual vigour, his ardent zeal, his love of truth, and the soundness and orthodoxy of the views which he so firmly held, and which he advocated with such clearness and courage. The name of Athanasius, the Deacon of Alexandria, had grown into a name of power and eminence. We cannot, therefore, be surprised at any distinction or honour that might be conferred upon him. He had clearly proved himself equal to any position in the Church to which, in God's providence, he might be called. Whatever exception might be taken against him on the score of youthfulness, none was admissible on the ground of incapacity or want of power. An event shortly occurred, which formed a great epoch in the life of Athanasius. Alexander, his chief pastor, friend, and earliest teacher, is said to have died within five months of his receiving the Meletian sectaries into the communion of the Church in accordance with the decree of the Council (see "Apol. c. Arian.," 59), which event, if it took place at the close of the Council, would fix the date of his death in January, 326 A.D. It can scarcely be placed later than April 17th or 18th, of that same year, which period would be in agreement with the Coptic chronology. The year 328 A.D. is given in the "Index" of the lately-discovered "Festal Letters" of St. Athanasius, but this date cannot be made to coincide with the language of Athanasius in his "Apology," unless we suppose that the reception of the Meletians was postponed for two years after the close of the Nicene Council, which is a very improbable supposition; nor, it may be added, is the chronology given in the "Index" much to be relied upon. It would appear that Alexander had already fixed the time, according to the scientific calculations of the Alexandrian astronomers, for the commencement of Lent and the Festival of Easter, which he, as Bishop of Alexandria, was appointed by the Nicene Council to determine. Of this period, when decided on, he gave information, in the first place, to his own diocese by means of a "Festal Letter," and afterwards sent instructions as to the date to the Bishop of Rome, with the request that he would convey the information to the remoter dioceses of his see.

The last moments of Alexander have an affecting interest in connexion with Athanasius. When the time of his death drew near, he is reported, in the presence of

the clergy who were gathered round his bed, to have
called for Athanasius; and when, in his absence, another
of the clergy who had the same name answered for him,
the dying bishop was said to have ignored this reply, and
again to have called for Athanasius, saying at the same
time, "You fancy that you will escape, but it cannot be"
(Soz., ii. 17; Theod, ii. 26). Two different accounts are
given of the cause of Athanasius's absence at this
particular time. One account says that Athanasius had
been sent by his bishop to the Court of the Emperor for
the transaction of some special mission (Epiph.
"Hæres.," lxix.). Another, and a more probable account
is, that Athanasius quitted the city, at the time of the
extreme illness of Alexander, through fear lest he should
be nominated to the vacant office on his patron's death.
From the history of St. Augustine, and other Fathers of
the Church, we are aware how often those who had
reason to imagine that they might be elected to the
Episcopal office, absented themselves, employing every
kind of expedient to escape the responsibility which they
feared might be thrust upon them.

It would appear that a considerable time intervened
between the death of Alexander and the consecration of
his successor. We are told by Arian authorities that
seven bishops—notwithstanding their vow openly to
elect the archbishop in a public place of meeting—laid
their hands in secret upon. Athanasius, and elected him
privately to the high office. Another version of his
consecration is also given by Arian adversaries. They
say (cf. Philostorgius, ii. 2) that Athanasius himself took
possession of the church of St. Dionysius late in the
evening, and having constrained two bishops who were
there to consecrate him, in spite of remonstrances and
anathemas, obtained by deceit the Emperor's

confirmation of the act, and then made use of the power of the State to punish those who held aloof from communion with him (Soz., ii. 17).

But some few years later we find that an Encyclic from the Egyptian bishops formally testified that a majority of them had publicly, in the presence of the laity of Alexandria, and with their openly expressed assent and approval, appointed Athanasius to the bishopric. It is added, that for many days and nights the people of Alexandria had been instant in their demands that Athanasius should be elected, asserting that he was likely to make both a good, and pious, and genuine bishop, and uttering aloud their prayers that he might be consecrated. It could hardly be supposed, remarks Gibbon, that the bishops would have given their solemn attestation to "a *public* falsehood."

Accordingly the wishes and demands of the people were gratified; and thus, to use the words of Gregory, "by the suffrages of the whole people, and not by those vile methods, afterwards prevalent, of force and bloodshed, but in a manner apostolic and spiritual, was Athanasius elevated to the throne of St. Mark."

The date of his consecration was probably the 8th of June, in the year 326 A.D.

Athanasius was now raised to be the representative of the Egyptian Church; and it is the assertion of Gregory Nazianzen, that "The Head of the Alexandrian Church is the Head of the world" ("Orat." 21). In his own province his jurisdiction was said to be even more extensive than that of the Roman Pontiff. He consecrated all the bishops throughout the entire diocese; and no bishop possessed an independent power of ordination. In the affairs of State and of civil polity the Bishop of Alexandria stood on an equality with a sovereign prince. The Patriarch of Alexandria (observes Gibbon, ch. xlvii.) "at a distance from court, and at the head of an immense capital, had gradually usurped the state and authority of a civil magistrate, and the Prefects of Egypt were awed or provoked by the Imperial power of these Christian Pontiffs."

CHAPTER VIII
"A Time of Peace." —(Eccles. 3:8)

We have seen Athanasius raised to the highest dignity in the Church in the greatest city of the world, next to Rome itself—a city which even outstripped its imperial rival in its commercial activity and wealth. It was confessedly a lofty position for so young a man to hold—one who had risen by a single bound, so to speak, from the office of deacon to that of archbishop.

But could Athanasius have looked into the future, he would have seen that, notwithstanding his remarkable elevation in the Church, days of storm and tempest lay before him, and that but very few peaceful hours were to be his portion in life. Could he have foreseen what was about to befall him, even his bold and undaunted spirit would have trembled at the sight.

A short breathing-space was, however, in the course of Providence, granted him at the outset of his career as bishop. For a brief moment he was allowed, quietly and without molestation, to carry out the work which he had so much at heart, namely, the evangelisation of the heathen, and the edification of the Christian Church.

(1.) The event that is said to have occurred almost

immediately after his appointment to the episcopate, contains an element of romance in the midst of what is deeply interesting and even affecting. Many of its details we learn from a Church historian who gathered them from the verbal testimony of one of the active agents in the events themselves (see Rufinus, i. 9; and cf. Soc. i. 19, and Soz. ii. 24).

We are told, and, as it would appear from what has just been stated, on trustworthy and reliable evidence, that as Athanasius was one day sitting in conference with some of his suffragan bishops, a man who had very recently come to Alexandria from Ethiopia or Abyssinia, (called by Socrates "India") requested an audience. When admitted, he informed the bishop that his name was Frumentius, and that he and his brother Ædesius, who were Christians, had accompanied, in their boyhood, for the sake of instruction, a relative of theirs, a philosopher of the name of Meropius or Moripius, from their native Tyre to Ethiopia. On their return home—such was the tale—the vessel on which they were sailing had put into a port on the Red Sea: and when there they were attacked by the savage inhabitants of the district, and all, with the exception of themselves, were cruelly massacred. It was said that the two boys were sitting down under the shelter of a tree by the shore preparing their work, and that the savages were touched at the sight, and spared their lives. Frumentius added that he and his brother were sold as slaves to the king of that region, and had been advanced by him to positions of trust and confidence, and that his brother Ædesius had been made the royal cup-bearer. He proceeded to say, that, on the death of the king, he had been appointed guardian to his son, and that he had done all that lay in his power to provide churches for the

worship of the Christian traders, who were living among
the people, and that he had also endeavoured to
promote the evangelisation of the natives of the country.
Moreover, Frumentius mentioned that the youthful king
had now taken on himself the functions of royalty; and
that, on their own request and desire, they were now
returning back again to the Roman Empire, though
anxiously urged to stay by the young king and his
mother. Ædesius had hurried forward to his home; but
he said that he could not justify himself in withholding
from the Alexandrian Church and Bishop a report of the
present condition of Ethiopia, and he prayed Athanasius
that a bishop might be sent to complete the work which
he had been permitted to initiate.

Athanasius, deeply interested in the narrative, at
once exclaimed—Who could be more fit than
Frumentius himself to become the first bishop of the
Abyssinian Church? Accordingly, with the sanction of
the other prelates who were present, Frumentius was
forthwith consecrated to the episcopal office (Theod., i.
23).

Frumentius, therefore, returned once more to
Abyssinia, made Axum his head-quarters, and was
maintained in his new sphere by the liberality of the
king, by whom he was deeply valued. His name for
many ages was highly honoured in the Church of
Abyssinia. In that Church he was named
"Fremonatos"—the name of "Saloma" being also given
him—and his memory was long cherished as one who
had "kindled in Ethiopia the splendour of the light of
Christ."

(2.) But shortly afterwards another event took place,
which, though of a comparatively peaceful character,
did not equal the one just recorded in its entire freedom

from all doctrinal controversy.

About this time—so we gather from Epiphanius ("Hæres.," lxix. 11), though Tillemont (viii. 30) has fixed a later date for the occurrence—Athanasius made a visitation in the district of the Thebaid. Anxiety was felt in that region not only from the conduct of the Arians, but also in consequence of the Meletian sectaries, who had resisted all the efforts of the Bishop of Alexandria to induce them to cease from holding themselves aloof from the Church, although he had zealously urged them to unity and uniformity.

From the severity of their morals the Meletians were held in no little estimation by the people, and from their opposition to the orthodox party, they were courted by the Arians. Though the Meletians were at first sound in their creed, and opponents of Arius, yet alter a while they united with the Arians in opposing and traducing Athanasius, so that he was led to remark ("Orat. c. Arian.," i.), that as Herod and Pontius Pilate forgot their enmity and joined together in persecuting Christ, so, in like manner, the Meletians and Arians concealed their private differences and animosities, and entered into a mutual league against the truth—a line of conduct to which history furnishes many parallels.

We are told that the well-known Pachomius—who was the great founder of monasteries in Egypt, and whose "rule" (Soz., iii. 14) was adopted throughout the East, as we may learn from the early life of Chrysostom—on the arrival of the archbishop, issued from his monastic institution at Tabenne, attended by a train of monks, to salute the Patriarch of Alexandria.

Fearing, however, lest he might be compelled to enter the priesthood by the archbishop, Pachomius hid himself amongst his attendant monks and others, who

had gathered there to see the occupant of the
"Evangelical throne," and looked with reverence—
unseen and undistinguished himself—on his famous
diocesan, in whom he recognised an earnest and zealous
servant of the Lord, ready to endure hardness in his
Master's service.

Egypt was, as is well known, in its earliest ages the
"fruitful parent of superstition;" and, subsequently, in
the loneliness of its deserts Antony fixed his dwelling-
place on the east of the Nile. In the sandy wastes of
Libya, amidst the gloomy rocks of Thebais, or the cell-
covered mountain of Nitria, or in the Island of Tabenne,
monks and anchorites and hermits abounded.
Pachomius founded numerous monasteries, and we hear
that sometimes at the Feast of Easter 50,000 persons
would gather together, who were obedient to his rule.

The dress of the Egyptian monks was strange and
fantastic. By the rule of Tabenne the monks were
precluded, except in extreme cases, from either bathing
their bodies in water, or anointing them with oil. They
slept either on the bare ground, or on a rough blanket or
mat. Their food was most spare, and of the simplest
kind; their only drink was water; they laboured in the
field or in the garden for their daily bread; their lives
were spent in solitude and in penance; they were
aroused to devotion during the night by the blast of the
horn, "which twice interrupted the vast silence of the
desert;" they dishonoured their bodies, inflicting upon
them the most grievous burdens and tortures; until at
length the name of Simeon Stylites was immortalised by
what Gibbon (ch. xxxvii.) has sarcastically termed the
"singular invention of an aërial penance."

Antony—whose name it has been said, was not so
much that of a person as of a power—was born in the

year 251 A.D., and lived till 356 A.D., a life of 105 years. He was, therefore, born 45 years before Athanasius, and died only 17 years before him. He has been commonly named the Father of Monasticism, but "not of such monasticism" (as a friendly critic has remarked) "as lives only for itself, but of such as trains many scholars, and seeks for spiritual strength by communion with God in solitude, in order to act upon kings and people, and upon cities and churches, in defence of the truth" (Bp. Wordsworth, "C. H.," i. 430). The same writer adds—"In contemplating, therefore, as we do with wonder, the unflinching faith, courage, and patience of St. Athanasius, and the battle which he fought almost single-handed for the truth for forty years, we ought not to forget the moral and spiritual comfort and support which he derived from the saintly eremite of Egypt."

CHAPTER IX
False Charges Against Athanasius

The quiet days of Athanasius were soon past and over. The bravery which he had displayed at the Nicene Council in opposing Arianism had raised up against him a host of embittered enemies, relentless in their hostility, and incapable of forgiveness. They scarcely ever allowed him from the time of his consecration to the last hour of his life a single day of undisturbed repose. Scheme succeeded scheme, and plot followed plot. Accusations against him on the part of the Arians never ceased.

(1.) It was about the year 330 A.D., that a plot was laid against him by Eusebius of Nicomedia, who induced the Emperor Constantine the Great to share in the persecution directed against the Bishop of Alexandria. When under the influence of antagonist views Constantine's character was unsettled and vacillating.

We have already seen in the letter addressed to Athanasius and Arius previous to the Nicene Council—in which the Emperor had urged them to settle their doctrinal dispute amicably for the good of the Church—that he had displayed an entire indifference towards

either side in the controversy, and had maintained, in
fact, a calm neutrality. But when a definite line of
teaching had been authorised by the Nicene Council,
and a dogmatic statement of the question at issue had
been formulated, the Emperor at once ceased to
maintain a neutral and negative position, and forthwith
took the side advocated by the Council. In the first
instance he had probably been much influenced by
Eusebius in standing aloof from the extreme views on
either side, in fact, from any definite avowal of opinion,
thinking that such a neutrality was more consistent with
State policy. But when a specific doctrine was formally
laid down by a great Council, of which he himself was
President, then it must have appeared to him that he had
no choice left, and that it became his duty to carry out
scrupulously the decrees of that Council. This transition
in his course of conduct does not appear either strange
or unnatural. He would, as a Roman Emperor, think
that the law ought to be upheld, and its decisions
obeyed.

He now desired that peace should be established in
the Church, even though it were necessary to enforce the
obedience of the Arians by penal enactments. In
carrying out this new resolution on his part he would,
very naturally, come into collision with his late friend
and spiritual confidant, Eusebius of Nicomedia. The
result of this clashing of opinions was, that Eusebius and
Theognius of Nicæa were both sent into exile at the
same time—the Emperor writing a letter to the people of
Nicomedia in explanation of his action against their
bishop.

But very soon the prelates procured their recall from
exile by making a profession of orthodoxy. Nor was this
all. It would seem probable that Eusebius was also

instrumental in obtaining the recall of Arius himself, who vindicated his character and views by the same kind of subterfuge, and concealment of his real opinions under a deceptive use of language and an equivocal phraseology, as that which Eusebius himself had employed. By such abuse of terms and definitions the unlearned were deceived, and real opinions were disguised and concealed.

It is recorded that Constantine once sent for Arius to his palace, and asked him plainly whether he agreed to the Nicene decrees, and that he, without any hesitation, subscribed. He expressed his readiness also to swear to this belief. Socrates (i. 8), however, relates that he had heard that Arius had under his arm a written statement of his real views, and that he swore that he believed as he had written! It must, however, be conceded, that the testimony for this barefaced equivocation is of a somewhat doubtful character.

According to Socrates (i. 25, 26), this change in the Emperor's opinions respecting Arius was brought about by means of an Arian presbyter, who exerted great influence over the mind of Constantia, the sister of Constantine, and the widow of Licinius. The Emperor is said to have placed his will in the hands of this same presbyter, with instructions that it should only be delivered over to Constantius. Constantia; during her last illness, commended this presbyter to her brother. He was in consequence admitted into close intimacy with the Emperor, and induced him to recall Arius, on the ground that he was an injured man, whose views were misunderstood and misrepresented. Socrates gives us the Emperor's letter of recall, which included the restoration of Euzoius also, whom Alexander had deposed from the office of deacon. They were admitted into the presence of Constantine, and made a profession of their belief in the Trinity. Their profession of faith is given by Socrates, who received it from Rufinus. The story, it must be allowed, has not the sanction of Valesius, who says that Athanasius takes no notice of it, but it is credited by the Benedictine editor. At this time it would seem that Constantine not only admitted Arius into his presence at Constantinople, but also gave him permission to return to Alexandria, of which permission, according to Socrates (i. 27), he actually availed himself. Constantine, moreover, is said to have written to Athanasius, requiring him to receive Arius into communion. This, however, Athanasius declined to do, even though threatened in an angry letter with expulsion from his diocese, if he still refused to comply with the Emperor's wishes.

Upon this the Eusebians formed a coalition with the Meletians, and together brought various accusations of a frivolous nature against Athanasius, in order to damage his reputation with Constantine.

(2.) But more than this was done by the enemies of Athanasius. A definite compact was now entered into with the Meletians of Egypt, of whom at this time John Arcaph was bishop and head. They were at length induced to promise their devoted assistance, whenever it might be needed. But the indictments against Athanasius were not to be of a theological character. To oppose the decisions of the Council of Nicæa would be ruinous to their plans. Other schemes must be devised. Eusebius was too shrewd a tactician to bring himself into collision with the bulk of the religious world, and with the majority of the bishops. He wrote, therefore, to the Bishop of Alexandria, pressing upon him the justice as well as the expediency of re-admitting Arius to

Church privileges, since his views had been
misinterpreted and his principles misunderstood. There
was a degree of menace underlying the mode in which
he made his appeal to Athanasius. But the answer of
Athanasius showed no signs of indecision or irresolution
in his maintenance of what he deemed to be truth. He
grounded his reply upon a twofold basis. He averred in
the first place that it would be a violation of all principle
to receive into the privileges of Church communion
those who had devised an heretical scheme of doctrine,
inconsistent with the truth; and, secondly, that by so
doing, they would appear to justify views which were
solemnly and deliberately anathematised at the Nicene
Council. Such was the strong ground upon which
Athanasius took up his position, and from which it
might readily be seen that he was not likely to be driven.

(3.) But Eusebius was too determined and too wily an
opponent to be easily driven from his object. Having
failed in his personal appeal to Athanasius, he brought a
higher influence to bear upon him. He appealed to the
intimacy which he still enjoyed with the Emperor, and
induced him to write a letter to Athanasius, which we
read in the pages of Socrates (i. 27), authoritatively
ordering Athanasius to receive into Church communion
all who desired to be admitted, under pain of expulsion
from his bishopric, if contumacious.

But even this Imperial missive did not move
Athanasius from the position which he had taken up,
and which he believed to be the only one that he could
conscientiously maintain. He, therefore, unflinchingly
informed Constantine that the Catholic Church could
not possibly hold communion with those who
advocated a heresy which, in fact, endeavoured to
overthrow the doctrine of the eternity and divinity of the

Son of God—a heresy which was deliberately fighting against Him. Thus Constantine must have found to his surprise, that a mandate was steadily resisted by a single bishop of the Church, which would have met with instantaneous obedience throughout the Empire, whatever consequences it might have involved. It would appear that, at least for the present, the Emperor was satisfied with Athanasius's reply; though from remarks which occur at the opening of the bishop's "Festal Letter" of 331 A.D., there would still seem to exist some causes of annoyance and vexation.

"Events," says a Church historian, "proved that Athanasius had a clear foresight of what that reception of the Arians involved; and though he was denounced by many as severe, and was persecuted as intolerant, yet it afterwards was manifest that he was actuated by the noblest motives of fervent zeal for God's glory, and of tender love for the salvation of souls."

(4.) But Eusebius was not idle; nor did his ill-will cease to urge him forward to make fresh charges against Athanasius. They may have been frivolous and easily refuted, but still they could not fail to prove annoying and irritating to the Archbishop.

Prompted by Eusebius, three Meletians—Eudæmus, Ision, and Callinicus—presented themselves to the Emperor, who was at this time at Nicomedia, and charged Athanasius with wrongfully usurping the authority which was only vested in the Imperial Government, by venturing to lay an impost on the people, in order to supply the Alexandrian Church with the linen tunics or albs, called "Sticharia," used in the services of the Sanctuary. It happened, however, that two priests of the Alexandrian Church, Alypius and Macarius, were at Court at that very time, and were able, satisfactorily, to refute the accusation made against the bishop. The Emperor, seeing how utterly unfounded was the charge made against Athanasius, wrote him a letter, in which he condemned the authors of the false indictment, and bade the bishop appear at Nicomedia.

(5.) In no way baffled by all the defeats which he had sustained, and urged on by implacable hostility, Eusebius induced Athanasius's accusers to bring forward against him, on his arrival at Nicomedia, a still more serious charge than had as yet been preferred against him. If proved guilty, he would be liable to be arraigned on a charge of high treason. For the indictment against him asserted, that he had sent a purse of gold to a rebel named Philumenus (Theod., i. 26). It is said that the Emperor heard this accusation against him in person, in the suburb of Nicomedia, which was called Psammathia. But this accusation—like those before it—the bishop was easily able satisfactorily to refute. The Emperor upon this sent Athanasius back to Alexandria, with a letter to the members of the Church there, in which he said that their bishop had been falsely and calumniously accused (Theod., i. 27; and "Con. Arian.," ch. lxi.).

(6.) Then followed the well-known tradition of the shattered chalice. There was a man of the name of Ischyras, who had for some time represented himself as a presbyter, although he had been declared by a Council at Alexandria to be a layman, since he had not been ordained by a bishop, but only by a presbyter named Colluthus, who was not in communion with the Church. Ischyras, nevertheless, persevered in taking clerical duty in a small village in the Mareotis, which was called the "Peace of Sancontarurum." The Mareotic region, according to Socrates, was very populous, containing many villages and churches, under the jurisdiction of the bishop of Alexandria. In this village Ischyras had a very small following, which included his father and some other near relations, the services being conducted in the residence of an orphan boy. Athanasius, who was carrying on a visitation in the district, having heard of this irregularity, sent a priest named Macarius, together with the parish priest of the district, to bid Ischyras appear before his bishop. On arriving there, they discovered that Ischyras was too unwell to attend the summons; they conveyed, therefore, the bishop's censure, through the agency of the father of Ischyras.

But on his recovery—his friends declining after this to join him any longer—Ischyras attached himself to the Meletians, who were pleased at being able to secure a standing in the Mareotis. The Meletians, however, resolved to make use of him as their instrument, and compelled him, by violence and intimidation, to declare that Macarius had found him in church in the act of "offering the oblations," and had thrown to the ground the Holy Table, fractured the chalice, and burned the church books. Of this sacrilegious act on the part of Macarius, his presbyter, the bishop, was to some extent to bear the blame. But Athanasius was able convincingly to establish before Constantine, at the suburb of Nicomedia called Psammathia, that all these allegations were false. There was, in the first place, no church in the village. Had there been one, there would have been no celebration of the Holy Communion on this day, since it was an ordinary week-day, even if Ischyras had been well enough to officiate, which he was not, but was confined to his bed in his cell. Moreover, he could not legitimately perform the function, since he was not rightfully ordained.

Athanasius gives us two accounts of the result of this indictment, one in his "Apology," and another in his fourth "Festal Letter" from the Court, in the beginning of the year 332 A.D. He informs his Egyptian brethren that he had suffered from protracted illness, but he tells them with satisfaction that the Meletians had been proved guilty of wilful and deliberate slander, and had been driven away with ignominy. Athanasius came back to Alexandria about the middle of Lent, and was the bearer of a letter from Constantine, in which he was very honourably spoken of, and his opponents censured. On his return, Ischyras besought the bishop, but in vain, to readmit him to Church privileges, asserting that the Meletians had compelled him to utter the falsehood. In the presence of thirteen of the clergy he denied the truth of the statement he had made, affirming that he had made it under fear and menaces.

CHAPTER X
Graver Plots Against Athanasius

Many of the charges—false and futile in themselves—have been recounted, which were directed against Athanasius at the commencement of his archiepiscopate. But plots of a more serious character followed each other in rapid succession. "Crimes" (says Hooker, "Ec. Pol." v. 42.2) "there were laid to his charge many, the least whereof being just had bereaved him of estimation and credit with men while the world standeth. His judges evermore the selfsame men by whom his accusers were suborned. Yet the issue always on their part, shame; on his, triumph."

(1.) John Arcaph, the Meletian Primate, again comes forward. He induces a Meletian bishop named Arsenius to hide himself away. A report was then disseminated that he had not only been murdered, but that he had also been dismembered by Athanasius for magical purposes. In attestation of this report, the Meletians displayed in a wooden box, with assumed grief, the dissevered hand of a man (Soc., i. 27; Soz., ii. 25; and Theod., i. 30).

This marvellous story reached the Emperor's ears;

and, strangely enough, he was induced to regard it as a
fitting matter for investigation. The Bishop of
Alexandria shortly after received a summons from the
Censor Dalmatius, Constantine's half-brother, to
proceed to Antioch, in order to stand his trial there …
Eusebius and Theognius were also sent by the Emperor
to Antioch to be present at the investigation. In the first
instance the bishop treated the matter with the contempt
that it deserved. He was, it has been supposed, at this
time away from Alexandria, engaged on a visitation in
Pentapolis and Ammoniaca. But afterwards he wrote to
the Egyptian clergy, and despatched a deacon to look
for the hiding-place of Arsenius. The deacon went at
once to the Thebaid, knowing that that was the country
of Arsenius, and discovered that he was lying in
concealment at Ptemencyrcis, in a monastery there,
which was situated on the east bank of the Nile. Before,
however, the deacon could reach the spot, Pinnes, the
superior of the monastery, had received intimation of
the search, and had sent Arsenius away into Lower
Egypt. The superior was arrested by the deacon, and
brought up before one of the "Dukes" of Egypt at
Alexandria, and was compelled to acknowledge in a
letter—written to John Arcaph, but which was probably
intercepted by some friend of the bishop and shown to
him—that Arsenius had never been murdered, but was
alive at that time. A diligent search was then made for
the man who was reported to be dead, and his discovery
was effected in an accidental manner. The servants of a
consular at Tyre happened to hear it mentioned at an
inn there, that Arsenius was concealed at some house in
the town. They carefully noticed the face of the man
who mentioned the circumstance, and told the consular.
The hint thus dropped was taken up. The house named

was searched, and a man was discovered hiding there, who declared that he was not the person sought for, until he was brought into the presence of Bishop Paul, who had been previously acquainted with Arsenius. His identity was then clearly ascertained. The Emperor, when he heard of this discovery, immediately quashed the proceedings at Antioch, and wrote at once a letter to Athanasius, which was to be made public, in which a warning was given to the Meletians, that any further acts of theirs, of such a kind as this, would be brought before the Emperor himself, and the matter would be dealt with as a question of civil law. At this time, also, Athanasius received a letter from Alexander, the old Bishop of Thessalonica, who had been present at the Council of Nicæa, congratulating him that Arcaph, whom he called the calumniator, had been brought to shame. Arcaph, however, was received into Church communion, after having expressed contrition and repentance for what he had done, and wrote to Constantine to announce his having been reconciled to Athanasius. Arsenius also sent to the bishop—not only in his own name, but also in that of the clergy—a renunciation of the schism of which he confessed himself to have been guilty, and made a formal promise of obedience to the Church over which Athanasius presided,—a promise which he observed in the future.

(2.) But notwithstanding these professions of regret and promises of amendment on the part of some of his opponents, the malevolence of other enemies of his was in no respect pacified or even mitigated. Again Eusebius comes forward. He induces the Emperor to believe that such serious charges as those recently brought against Athanasius could only be satisfactorily inquired into by a council. He mentioned Caesarea—where one of his own name was bishop, who had already favoured the cause of Arianism—as a suitable place for the meeting of the council. In accordance with his suggestion, a council was summoned to meet there at the commencement of the year 333 A.D. It was clear to Athanasius that he could expect no justice at a council held at such a place, and under such adverse circumstances; and, accordingly, for two years and a half (Soz. ii. 25) he refused to attend. In consequence of this refusal, he was regarded as contumacious, and received an imperious order from the Emperor to attend at a council which was about to sit at Tyre, some short time before the intended consecration of the Church of the Resurrection at Jerusalem. Thither Athanasius went in the summer of the year 335 A.D., accompanied by nearly fifty of his suffragan bishops from Egypt, who were indignant at being introduced into the council not, as was usual, by deacons, but by a "Registrar of Indictments," and entered also a formal protest through Athanasius against certain bishops being present at the council who were open partisans of the Arian cause. The assembly was a large one. Sixty Eastern bishops met at Tyre, besides the forty-seven Egyptian bishops who came with Athanasius. These sixty were principally Eusebians. Among them were Eusebius of Nicomedia, Eusebius of Cæsarea, Placillus of Antioch, Theognius of Nicæa, Theodore of Heraclea, Maris of Chalcedon, Ursacius of Singidunum, and Valens of Mursa in Pannonia. There were a few bishops of the orthodox party there, viz., Maximus of Jerusalem, Alexander of Thessalonica, Asclepas of Gaza, and Marcellus of Ancyra. It was at once evident to Athanasius, that the majority of those present were supporters of Arian views. The bishop who presided, Placillus or Flacillus of

Antioch, had derived his appointment from the Arian party. Athanasius saw his trusted priest, Macarius, brought up before the council by a military guard in chains. He himself had to stand up as a defendant Potammon, an aged Egyptian bishop, who had been present at the Council of Nicæa, and who had been deprived of one of his eyes in the persecution under Maximian, indignantly asked Eusebius of Cæsarea, how he ventured to sit in judgment on the innocent Athanasius? (Epiph. "Hær." 69). Count Dionysius—appointed by the Emperor to keep order in the assembly—inclined to the Arian side. Ischyras, also, might be seen in the council amongst the bishop's accusers. In addition to the former charges brought against him, some fresh ones were added, of which some related to the circumstances connected with his election to the See of Alexandria. The base charge of immorality shamefully preferred against him, but triumphantly refuted by Timotheus his presbyter, may be passed over in silence. Though opponents convicted of slander were listened to, yet his own suffragans were hot allowed to give evidence in his favour without interruption and annoyance. Of these accusations many were at once disproved by Athanasius; in regard to others he requested time before replying to them. Once again the dead man's hand was exposed to view in the box, and a cry of sympathetic horror arose from his enemies at the sight. Upon this Athanasius asked with perfect calmness, whether any one in the assembly knew Arsenius? Many replied that they knew him. Then Athanasius introduced into the assembly a man, with eyes fixed upon the ground, and with his face closely covered up. He bade him raise his head and look at the assembly. When he had done so, Athanasius asked, is

not this Arsenius? His identity could not for a moment
be denied. The bishop then drew from under the cloak
in which Arsenius was enveloped, first one hand, and
then—after a pause—another, observing with caustic
irony and sarcastic humour, "I presume that no one
thinks that God has given to any man more than two
hands"! (cf. Soc., ii. 29; Soz., ii. 25; Theod., i. 28).
Confusion naturally followed such an exposure of the
falsity of the charge brought against Athanasius. Arcaph
himself hurriedly quitted the meeting. Some, however,
of his confederates, with greater astuteness, exclaimed
that all this was the result of magical contrivance and
deception, and created against Athanasius such a
manifestation of irrational frenzy and excitement, that
the bishop was only preserved from their frantic violence
by the interposition of Dionysius in his behalf.

(3.) The matter of the broken chalice still remained to
be cleared up to the satisfaction of the members of the
council. They consequently determined to send
commissioners to the Mareotis to inquire still more fully
into the subject. Notwithstanding the protest of the
Egyptian bishops, six commissioners were despatched
by the council, all of whom were undisguised Eusebians;
viz., Theognius of Nicæa, Maris of Chalcedon,
Theodore of Perinthus, Macedonius of Mopsus in
Cilicia, Ursacius of Singidunum in Mæsia, and Valens
of Mursa in Pannonia. The two last-named had in their
earlier days been instructed by Arius, and in
consequence degraded from the priesthood but they had
afterwards been appointed to bishoprics in Pannonia,
"for their impiety" (to use Athanasius's strong
expression) or, in other words, for their zealous efforts
in the cause of Arius.

The commissioners, accompanied by Ischyras, as one

of their party, commenced their investigation in the
Mareotis. They allowed professed unbelievers to give
evidence respecting the Table and the Chalice, but
excluded presbyters. The Prefect of Egypt, Philagrius,
who had apostatized to Arianism, was present with his
soldiers, for the purpose of overawing and intimidating
those who gave witness. We find that both Jews and
Catechumens were permitted to bear testimony, though
neither of these classes could have been present at the
celebration of the Holy Communion. Still, these
interested and partial witnesses could not testify to any
books having been burnt, nor could they contradict the
evidence brought forward to prove that Ischyras had (as
he himself had once allowed) been too ill at the time to
be present at the service at which the sacrilegious acts
were said to have been committed. Such a one-sided and
partisan inquiry, as Arsenius himself afterwards
admitted it to be, was indignantly objected to by the
Alexandrian and Mareotic clergy. The commissioners,
in defiance of all protests, when they had procured the
banishment of four priests of Alexandria, and permitted
the lowest of the people to ill-treat the Alexandrian
Christians before their eyes, even on a fast-day, went
back to Tyre.

Athanasius had made a complaint to Dionysius
immediately the commissioners started for Egypt,
alleging that the composition of the Court of Inquiry
was unfair, and that its members were unduly biased in
one direction, and that the particular men to whom he
had made objection were sent there. The Archbishop's
suffragans also made an earnest appeal, urging that the
case should be reserved for the Emperor's special
hearing. Some of them also passionately complained to
Alexander of Thessalonica, that "the wild beasts were

about to rush upon them." Upon this Alexander addressed a letter to Dionysius, taking exception to the composition of the Court of Inquiry, and speaking of Athanasius as being the victim of a conspiracy. In consequence of this appeal, Dionysius felt himself constrained to address a letter to the Eusebians, praying them not to suffer the decisions of the council to be nullified by injustice. Athanasius, however, was convinced in his own mind, that the acts of the council had already been vitiated by unfair conduct on the part of the Eusebians, and determined at once, without waiting for the decision of so packed an assembly, to make the daring experiment of seeing whether the Imperial throne could be reached by the voice of truth. Accordingly, accompanied by five of his Suffragans (Soc., i. 34; Soz., ii. 28; "Apol.," § 87), he at once took ship for Constantinople, and suddenly presented himself, taking his stand in the middle of the road before the Emperor when riding into the city. At first Constantine did not recognise the bishop; but when he learnt who he was, he endeavoured to pass him by in silence. Athanasius, however, did not stir from the position he had taken, and thus addressed the Emperor: "Either convene a legitimate assembly, or afford me an opportunity of meeting my accusers in your presence." The bishop's request was granted.

We learn that the members of the council, when they had received the report of their commissioners, condemned Athanasius,—recognised the Meletians as orthodox, and, after having gone to Jerusalem, on the summons of Marianus, the Secretary of the Emperor, to be present at the dedication of the splendid church there, called the Great "Martyrium" on Cavalry (see Soc., 133; Soz., ii. 26; Theod., i. 29; and Euseb., "V. C.," iii. 33–

39. and iv. 43, 45), declared Arius and Euzoius to be orthodox in their views, their opinion being based on a statement of Arius's doctrines which he had made five years before.

A Synodical Letter was addressed ("Apol." § 84) to the Alexandrian Church by the council, as well as to all bishops, in which it was stated that they had received letters from the Emperor to admit the Arians to Church privileges, on their profession of the orthodox faith, and that they had complied with his instructions.

(4.) We can readily understand that after this the Eusebians must have been not a little surprised and alarmed at receiving a letter from the Emperor, in which their conduct was looked upon with suspicion, and in which they were bidden to proceed at once to Constantinople. No inconsiderable number of them, in their excitement and fear, retired immediately to their respective homes; but others nominated as a deputation the following delegates to go to Constantinople, namely, the two Eusebii, Patrophilus, Theognius, Valens, and Ursacius, who boldly went to the Imperial Court, and passing over altogether the question of the commissioners' report, brought forward a new accusation, which, like most of the former ones, was of a semi-political character, namely, that Athanasius had spoken of coming distress to Constantinople, by hindering the sailing of the corn-vessels from Alexandria, a charge which was calculated to excite the indignation of Constantine, since it directly touched upon his prerogatives; a charge which even caused the death of the most distinguished of the heathen philosophic party, Sopater, the pupil of Iamblichus.

Athanasius asked, how could a private citizen, and far from wealthy, do anything of this sort? Eusebius of

Nicomedia replied—strengthening his words with an oath—that the bishop was a man of power, influence, and wealth, and able to do what he liked.

The Emperor, with an assumption of indignation in his manner, prevented Athanasius from defending himself. He may, perhaps, have entertained strong doubts as to the truth of the charges brought against the bishop, but yet he may have wished to be quit of the matter altogether, being weary of these never-ending controversies; and thus, as Socrates suggests, he may have persuaded himself that he was likely to promote peace and harmony in the empire and in the church by banishing Athanasius; or he may have desired to silence the bishop's accusers for his benefit, thinking that thus his life would be more likely to be preserved. Certainly when Constantine II. sent Athanasius back to Alexandria, he tells the Alexandrians in the letter he addressed to them, about two months after his father's death, that Constantine the Great had sent the bishop to Treves, to be out of the way of those designs upon his life which his embittered enemies were constantly attempting to carry out. From whatever motives Constantine may have acted—and his motives were not unfrequently difficult to discover—he abruptly ended the trial by sending the bishop, as an exile, to the far-off city of Trier or Treves, the capital of the first province of Belgium, where his eldest son, Constantine, held his court, and where the imperial viceroys had their residence. By this son the bishop was received with kindness and consideration, in February of the year 336 A.D.

It has been remarked that it was a fortunate thing for the Church that Athanasius, when thus banished for the first time, was sent into the West, and not as some other bishops, who were exiled in that century for their faith and courage, to some inhospitable region in the East. He was thus brought into contact with the two emperors of the West, Constantine the eldest, and Constans the youngest son of Constantine, and was able to exercise a salutary influence over them.

CHAPTER XI
Athanasius's First Exile Passed at Treves

Athanasius's exile at Treves lasted nearly two years and a half. It may seem a long period of enforced absence from his native city and his diocese; but it was an interval of rest, which probably he, like Chrysostom, much needed in the midst of all the storms and troubles of his agitated life. He required repose and strengthening as well in body as in spirit. He had already been called upon to pass through much suffering, labour, annoyance, and opposition; and he could not fail to see that there was much anxiety and danger awaiting him in the future. It was, however, an unwonted position for him to be placed in. Instead of energetic action, unceasing work, never-ending strain of body and of mind, constant effort and progress, he was now called upon to "sit still."

This was for some time to be his "strength." But it must have proved a strange and novel experience for him. He had left behind him the city of his birth and the scene of his labours,—a place endeared to him by innumerable associations; and he was transferred to a town in Gallia, far removed from everything which he had either seen, or of which he had heard. He was not, indeed, banished as Chrysostom was, to some wild, remote, and cheerless village, on the border-land of civilisation, in constant dread of banditti, and exposed to the chill blasts of the stormy wind which swept over the bleak and snowy mountain-ranges that rose all around him. The place selected for Athanasius's first exile was far different from this, and far more pleasant in itself. The city of Treves was one in which the Emperor Constantine the Great had frequently dwelt from 306 to 331 A.D., and in which, as we have seen, his eldest son Constantine was now residing. It was a city even then venerable from its antiquity, and one that might be regarded as Imperial. Its classical name, "Augusta Trevirorum," indicated its connexion with Rome. It was built on the right bank of the Moselle, and it was described by Ausonius, who wrote in the latter half of the fourth century, as fourth in his list of noble cities,—a rank to which it fairly laid claim, as being the headquarters of the Roman commanders on the Rhine, and the frequent imperial residence of the Cæsars in this division of Gallia. Constantine would appear to have rebuilt its walls. Its vast circus, its basilicæ, and its forum, were spoken of by Eumenius as royal works. The city stood on a somewhat level plain, surrounded with gently-sloping hills, which were clad with vines. A Roman bridge, probably the work of Agrippa, of nearly 700 feet in length and 21 feet in width, spanned the Moselle, the massive foundations of which alone exist. One gate remains, called the "Porta Martis," or, as it was named in the Middle Ages, the "Porta Nigra." It is a grand and vast quadrangular building, four storeys in height on one of its flanks, composed of huge blocks of stone, with two gateways in the central portion, and with large chambers over the gateways. It is a work of the most imposing architectural character and proportions, and of very great defensive strength. The remains of the amphitheatre, which was originally within the walls, now lie without them; and the ruins of the ancient Thermæ are still very striking memorials of Roman beauty of architecture. Ammianus called the city "Domicilium principum clarum;" and to him the city presented in its architecture and buildings many evidences of Roman grandeur and magnificence in all their freshness and newness of execution, which the modern traveller can now trace only in their decay.

Such were some of the splendid specimens of Roman architecture, and signs of Roman imperialism, which Athanasius would have looked upon in his place of exile, with not unappreciative, though perhaps with saddened and homesick gaze. He would also have regarded with deep interest the vast church, not yet out of the builder's hands, used by the Christian inhabitants of the city on high festivals, portions of which are possibly incorporated in the present cathedral. Nor would the natural beauties of the place have escaped his keen observation,—its vine-clad hills, its lovely river, and its fertile plain.

His place of exile was not, therefore, without its attractiveness to his cultured mind and refined taste. Moreover, he tells us that he was supplied in abundance with all the necessaries of life; and in Maximin, the orthodox Bishop of Treves, he found a faithful friend and beloved companion. He had also around him some brethren from Egypt, whose intercourse and sympathy must have afforded him no little consolation; and he was allowed to carry on an extensive correspondence with his friends in Alexandria and elsewhere, though it was possible that his letters might be sometimes intercepted by his enemies for the purpose of discovering grounds of accusation against him.

We can well imagine him sitting by the gently-gliding waters of the calm Moselle, and thanking God and taking courage, when he heard how the Christian inhabitants of his native city had succeeded in opposing the return of Arius to Alexandria; or how the Emperor had received baptism just before his death in May, 337 A.D. Nor would he have dwelt with anything but gratified satisfaction on the efforts which his fellow-citizens, assisted by Antony, had made, in endeavouring to prevail upon the Emperor to grant their prayer for his return from exile, even though that prayer had not proved successful (Soz., ii. 31).

At this time—in his days of comparative quietness and peace—he wrote to the presbyters of Alexandria, urging them to enter fully into the Apostle's words, and to make them their own,—"Nothing shall separate us from the love of Christ." And still later on, at the beginning of the year 338 A.D., he addressed a "Festal Letter" to the Church, in which he assures his fellow-Christians that, though "absent in the flesh," he should still be "present in the spirit," and keep the Easter feast in heart with them ("Fest. Ep." 10). He also affectionately reminded them that the road to consolation often led through affliction; that God's saints must expect the opposition of the unbelievers; but that those whose life was hid in Christ would eventually gain the crown.

The death of Constantine the Great occurred in the beginning of the second year of his exile.

Constantine was preparing to make an expedition against Persia, but the Persians sent an embassy, and proposed conditions of peace. We learn that after Easter the health of Constantine, which had always been very robust, suddenly failed; and that he resorted to the warm baths of Constantinople, and then to Helenopolis, but that not being benefited by them, he removed from thence to Nicomedia, in Bithynia, A.D. 337. Conscious that his end was near, he resolved to receive the Holy Sacrament of Baptism. He had delayed it—so he said to the bishops who were with him—because he had desired to be baptised in the river Jordan, in which his Saviour had been baptised (Euseb. "V. C." iv. 62). After humbly confessing his sins at Helenopolis, he received baptism at the Villa Ancyrona, in a suburb of Nicomedia, at the hands of Eusebius the bishop of that city, assisted by other bishops. He was attired, says Eusebius the historian, in a white baptismal robe, which he wore till his death, never exchanging it for the purple. We are told that on Whitsunday, May 22nd, A.D. 337, about noon, after prayer and thanksgiving to Almighty God, Constantine expired. He is generally supposed to have been 63 years old at the time of his death, having reigned thirty-one years, which was the longest reign of any Roman Emperor since that of Augustus. His body having been laid out in state in a coffin of gold, covered with purple (Euseb., "V. C." iv. 66, 67, 70), was carried from Nicomedia to Constantinople, where it was placed on high in the noblest room of the palace, and was adorned with the imperial diadem and other insignia of royalty, and surrounded with burning tapers on golden candlesticks, and at length was buried by his second son Constantius, in the Church of the Holy Apostles at Constantinople.

The death of Constantine the Great did not affect, for another year, the condition of Athanasius in any appreciable degree. But in June, 338 A.D., Constantine II., who took a kind of precedency in the division of the empire over his brothers Constantius and Constans, wrote from Treves to the Church at Alexandria, stating to them his determination to send back—in compliance with his father's wishes and intention—Athanasius to his see, and expressing at the same time a very high opinion of his conduct and his character ("Apol.," 87). Constantine added that at Treves Athanasius had been supplied with all things needful, although his "illustrious virtue, trusting in the divine aid, lightly regarded the severest sufferings" ("Apol.," § 8).

It would seem that, in this step, he had reckoned on his brothers' agreement with him.

He accordingly took Athanasius in his company to Viminacium or Viminiacum, a town in Mæsia Superior, lying on the main road to Constantinople. At this important place the three Emperors met, and all agreed in the restoration of Athanasius to his bishopric. Athanasius, after passing through Constantinople, where he met Constantius, had a second interview with him at the Cappadocian Cæsarea.

Athanasius arrived in Alexandria in November, 338 A.D. He was received by the Church with sympathetic congratulation and rejoicing ("Apol. c. Arian." § 7).

In the different churches thanksgivings for his safe return were earnestly offered up, and his clergy declared that the day of his return was the happiest day in their lives. It was observed as an annual festival.

CHAPTER XII
Fresh Troubles on His Return to His See

Athanasius soon discovers that the animosity of his adversaries is unrelenting. Fresh charges are levelled against him. The Emperors are informed that he had wrongly appropriated the corn which the late Cæsar had given for purposes of charity to the widows in Egypt and Libya; and also that the day of his return to Alexandria had been marked by bloodshed. Athanasius, in consequence of these charges, received an angry letter from Constantius, who would appear to have believed in the truth of the former of the two accusations made against him. Athanasius, however, replied; and successfully refuted not only the first, but the second charge also ("Apol.," § 18; Soc., ii. 3; Soz., iii. 2). Most unhappily for the Bishop, Constantius—so speedily about to prove "his scourge and torment by all the ways that malice armed with sovereign authority could devise and use"—fell deeper and deeper under the baleful influence of Athanasius's persistent enemy, Eusebius of Nicomedia. He had just been translated to the See of Constantinople, which was rendered vacant by the second expulsion of Bishop Paul,—the successor of

Alexander, in 336 A.D.,—who was said to have been afterwards strangled in a gloomy cell at the lonely Cucusus in 352 A.D.

The Eusebians would appear first to have gained over to their side in the Court of Constantius the eunuch Eusebius, the great Chamberlain of the Palace, and then the Empress, and finally the facile, pliant, and credulous Emperor himself, who was still a young man, and whose opinions were unformed. They afterwards addressed letters full of malicious and untruthful accusations against the bishop to Constantine II. and Constans.

This period seemed a suitable one to the Eusebians for endeavouring to carry out a scheme which they could not effect during Constantine's lifetime, namely, the placing on the "Evangelical Throne" an Arian of the name of Pistus. He had been a priest when Alexander was bishop, and had been deposed by him for his advocacy of Arian views, but had been consecrated, so it was said, by a well-known Arian bishop of the name of Secundus. The Eusebians urgently asserted that Athanasius had violated the ecclesiastical law by being restored to his diocese by the civil power, when he had been expelled by a decree of the Council of Tyre. It seems strange and almost unaccountable, that men who had depended so greatly on the Imperial authority and on the support of the State, should bring forward such an accusation against Athanasius. No doubt he very fairly conceived that no weight could be attached to the decision of a council, which, by its manifest partiality and injustice, and the defects by which it was vitiated, both in its constitution and mode of procedure, had ceased to claim any respect or obedience.

Another petty annoyance was at this time inflicted on

Athanasius by the Eusebians, who had made Ischyras a bishop, and had procured the sanction of the Emperor that a church should be erected for him. The church was built, but we are informed ("Apol.," 12, 85), that he could not muster a congregation to fill it.

And now the Eusebians had recourse to another quarter, in order to obtain the necessary authority for placing Pistus over the Church of Alexandria. They applied to the head of the Western Church. They deputed three of their clergy—Macarius the presbyter, and the deacons, Martyrius and Hesychius—to wait upon Julius, the Bishop of Rome. Athanasius, being informed of this deputation, despatched certain presbyters to Rome, to plead his cause before the bishop. He sent out also a famous encyclic from the Synod, assembled in A.D. 340, at Alexandria, from the Thebaid, Libya, and Pentapolis, consisting, as Athanasius tells us, of close upon a hundred bishops. This valuable encyclic is extant, inserted in his "Apology against the Arians." He also despatched a private and personal letter to different bishops who espoused his cause and anathematized his rival Pistus. His presbyters at Rome gave such strong and convincing evidence in regard to Pistus, that the chief of the three envoys of the Eusebians, although suffering at the time from illness, departed hastily during the night. The remaining Eusebian envoys begged Julius to summon a Synod, and, if he were willing, to act as judge of the case. In accordance with this request, he summoned both sides to a Synod at some place on which Athanasius might fix.

But in the year 340 A.D., Athanasius was grieved to hear of the death of his kind friend and patron, Constantine II., the eldest of the three Imperial brothers, who was killed when invading the dominions of his brother Constans.

It was at this time announced that Pistus was set aside, and that a Cappadocian of the name of Gregory was sent by the Court to be installed Bishop of Alexandria. The bishopric would seem to have been first offered to Eusebius, of Edessa, named Emissenus (that is, Bishop of Emesa), but was declined by him, because he knew with what affection the people regarded Athanasius, and feared an outburst of popular fury (Soc., ii. 9; Soz., iii. 6). We learn from Athanasius that this nomination of Gregory to the bishopric was regarded as a scandalous proceeding by the Alexandrian Church.

The different churches were crowded with sorrowing and indignant worshippers, just as the churches of Antioch were afterwards similarly thronged, under parallel circumstances, in the days of Chrysostom. The Christian and orthodox population of Alexandria urged upon the authorities in the city, with all the excitement that a sense of wrong called forth, that this insult was directed against their lawful bishop by the mere spitefulness and hatred of the Arian faction. They were fully aware that Gregory was favourable to Arianism, and in consequence pleasing to the Eusebians; and, moreover, that he was a compatriot of Philagrius, the governor, who was naturally fierce and cruel, a Pagan in religion, and, what was worse, an apostate from the Christian faith (see Cave, p. 105.)

We are informed by Gregory Nazianzen that the intruding prelate had once studied in Alexandria, where he had been courteously treated by Athanasius. But all objections and expostulations were alike of no effect. Philagrius made an attack upon the Church of St.

Quirinus, and urged on the lowest of the people, and some rude inhabitants of the country district, to commit the most cruel and sacrilegious outrages. The church books were committed to the flames; the holy table was profaned by heathen sacrifices; the church stores were plundered; wild and drunken revels took place in the baptistry; and monks, virgins, and widows were ill-treated, and, in some cases, murdered. ("Hist. Arian.," § 10; "Apol.," § 30.)

At this time Athanasius had taken up his residence within the precincts of the Church of St. Theonas. He was well aware that the hostility and ill-feeling were really directed against him. In order, therefore, to prevent any further desecration or bloodshed, he resolved to quit the city, and to seek a place of concealment in the neigbourhood, at which he composed an "Encyclical Letter," giving an account of all the terrible miseries which had befallen the Alexandrian Church. This letter (according to Tillemont) bears upon it evident signs of the haste in which it was written. After the lapse of a few days, Gregory is said to have entered the city as bishop.

The season of Lent was disfigured by an Arian persecution. Gregory, enraged, it is said, at the loathing shown by the orthodox at his entering into a certain church, caused Philagrius, on Good Friday, to scourge thirty-four women, one of whom held a Psalter in her hand; and on Easter Day, to the satisfaction of the heathen population of the city, he imprisoned many orthodox believers. Some captains of ships were put to the torture in order to make them take Gregory's "Letters of Communion." The clergy were not allowed to visit the sick or to baptise; the laity could not pray undisturbed in their own houses; an indictment, in which Athanasius was charged with capital offences, which bore the signatures alike of heathens and Arians, was intrusted to Philagrius for presentation to the Emperor.

After completing and despatching in haste his Encyclic, in which he urged all bishops to unite in this, crisis, Athanasius sailed to Rome, probably in the Easter season of 340 A.D.,—though much difficulty prevails in respect to the chronology of this particular period,—and entered the city some weeks after the time when Constantine II. had been slain during his invasion of Italy.

Thus perished the royal benefactor of Athanasius. Constans, however, who thus became master of Gaul and Spain, and the countries north of the Alps, befriended him, and requested him to supply him with some copies of Holy Scripture for his use, which were accordingly sent to him from Alexandria. (Athan., "Apol.," § 4; Wordsworth's "Church Hist.," ii. 74, 5.)

CHAPTER XIII
His Second Exile Spent at Rome

Athanasius was received at Rome with all kindness by Julius, the bishop of the see. He was anxious, in the first instance, to submit his case for consideration to the Church of Rome; and, when he had done this, he spent most of his time in attending the religious services of the Church. He was also very kindly treated by Eutropion, the Emperor's aunt, and, amongst several others, by Abuterius and Sperantius. Moreover, he was cheered by the letters which he received from the friends whom he had left behind him in Egypt.

When Julius had welcomed Athanasius to Rome, he despatched two presbyters, Elpidius and Philoxenus, in the beginning of the summer of 340 A.D., to renew the invitation which he had given to the Eusebian bishops (Athan., "c. Arian.," § 20; "Hist, ad Mon.," § 11), to fix definitely upon the following December as the date of the proposed council; and to name Rome as the place where it should be held.

Athanasius was attended at Rome by two Egyptian monks, Isidore and Ammonius, famous for their sanctity, the latter of whom is said to have manifested no concern for any of the noted buildings of the seven-hilled city, except the church of St. Peter and St. Paul (Soc., iv. 23).

But much interest at Rome was concentrated upon them; and the enthusiastic admiration evinced by Athanasius for Antony and other monks would seem not only to have lessened the dislike felt at Rome for the monastic orders, but even to have excited a decided interest in their favour. It can scarcely be doubted that the three years of exile which Athanasius spent at Rome, not only tended to confirm the Latin Church in its orthodoxy of belief, from the influence which his masculine mind and remarkable genius exerted over it; but also produced a strong feeling among the members of the Church of Rome in favour of monastic institutions, so that Gibbon (iv. 308) uses such strong language as this:—"Athanasius introduced into Rome the knowledge and practice of the monastic life." On the other hand, it would have been remarkable if Athanasius's tone of mind and line of thought had not been influenced to a certain extent by this long period of exile passed in the western capital of the Roman empire. His mind was then, to a greater degree than it had ever been before, brought into contact with Roman thought, Roman manners, and Roman greatness. He could not fail to have observed the calm, practical, and deliberative tone of mind which prevailed among the intelligent classes in that ruling city of the world. He may, indeed, have been conscious of the greater vivacity, quickness of intellect, logical subtlety, and philosophic acuteness of the educated population of Alexandria. He may justly have felt that for such discussions as those with which he had been familiar, when analysing the subtle distinctions, real and verbal, which naturally presented themselves in the contemplation of the great doctrine of the Trinity, and for all the abstract speculations which grew around such a question, the keen intellect of the Greek or Alexandrian was the better instrument of thought; but he would not be able to shut out the conviction that the unexcited, deliberative, and unbiased logic of the Roman, would possess many advantages, and would exert much influence in curbing the tendency to extreme views, fantastic speculations, novel theories, and the taste for special pleading and casuistry, to which the Eastern Church was both naturally and nationally inclined.

As Athanasius wandered by the storied banks of the Tiber, or surveyed the mighty mass of the Colosseum, or as his eye rested upon the princely palaces which the Roman senators and consuls had raised, or as he gazed upon the Forum, "that monument of ancient power," of which he had heard and read so much, or on the Temple of Tarpeian Jove, or the vast public baths, or the magnificent Pantheon, he must have been impressed with similar feelings to those which Ammianus Marcellinus (xvi. 10) ascribes to Constantius, when he beheld the glories of the ancient city, telling us that the king was "confounded with astonishment," and that his feeling was that "rumour which commonly magnifies everything, had here shown itself weak and malignant, and had given but a feeble description of the wonders of Rome." Horace was true when he said:—

"Possis nihil urbe Româ
Visere majus."—(Carm. Sæc.)

During this same time, Elpidius and Philoxenus were actively engaged on their mission. When, however, the

Eusebian leaders were assured that the council to which they were invited would not be under imperial control, but would be a free and independent ecclesiastical synod, they managed to detain the envoys beyond the time fixed for the council, until January, 342 A.D., and then sent them back with the fictitious excuse that Constantius was occupied with his Persian war, and that impediments were thus thrown in the way of travelling. But the Eusebians did not confine themselves to such negative action as this. They urged on Philagrius the Prefect, and Gregory, the newly-installed Bishop of Alexandria, to the commission of fresh cruelties in that ill-fated city, now deprived of the services of its lawful bishop. Moreover, they expelled from his see Serapammon, both bishop and confessor; they inflicted on Bishop Potammon stripes so severe that he never recovered from the effects of them; and other bishops they condemned to imprisonment and different bodily sufferings.

The letters which Athanasius received when at Rome from his friends in Alexandria at this time must have cut him to the heart. They told a sad and never-ending tale of cruelties and tortures inflicted on the orthodox, of confiscation of their property, of bitter feeling evinced really towards himself in their ill-treatment of his aunt, and of the way in which Gregory gave his support and sanction to Duke Balacius, the commander of the Egyptian forces, who sat as assessor with Gregory in the Courts of Justice, and displayed a merciless and implacable cruelty to the followers of Athanasius, though warned by Antony to desist from such a course of conduct.

It was under the influence of such sad and discouraging accounts of the condition of the Christian population of that city, on which the deepest affections of his nature were centred, that he wrote his "Festal Letter" from Rome in the beginning of the year 341 A.D. In that letter Athanasius remarks:—"Although with afflictions and sorrows the opposers of Christ have oppressed you also together with us; yet, God having comforted us by our mutual faith, behold, I even write to you from Rome. Keeping the feast here with the brethren, still I also keep it with you in will and in spirit; for we send up prayers in common to God, 'Who hath granted us not only to believe in Him, but also now to suffer for His sake' (Phil. 1:29). For, troubled as we are, because we are so far from you, He moves us to write, that by a letter we might comfort ourselves, and provoke one another to good."

Athanasius had hoped that long ere this his own case would have been settled, but he was doomed to disappointment. No Council had yet been convened. The Eusebians had not presented themselves at Rome. At last the envoys arrived, the bearers of so insolent a letter from the Eusebians (Soc., ii. 15), that Julius refrained from reading it himself to the Church, hoping that perchance some of the party might still come, and that this might render the reading of it unnecessary, ("Apol." 24).

But no Eusebians came to Rome. They had, in fact, seized upon the opportunity afforded them by the dedication of the new cathedral at Antioch, called the "Golden Church," which had been left unfinished by Constantine, to convene a council there. According to Socrates its real object was to do away with the Nicene Confession of Faith, which the Eusebians despaired of accomplishing during the lifetime of Constantine. Accordingly, about August, 341, A.D.—as it has been supposed—a council named the "Synod of the Dedication." consisting, according to Sozomen, of ninety-seven bishops, was assembled. At this Council were present all the notorious leaders of the Arian party; but it is to be noticed that neither Maximus of Jerusalem was there, nor Julius of Rome, though Socrates adds (ii. 8), that it was in violation of ecclesiastical rule to pass canons without the sanction of the Bishop of Rome, and this Council published about twenty-five canons in relation to cases of order and discipline, some of them of primary importance, which were "received into the Code of the Canons of the Universal Church" (Wordsworth, "C. H.," ii. 81). So far as mere numbers were concerned, the orthodox party had a slight majority in their favour; but the Eusebians, backed up by imperial support, were in fact the more powerful. Many of them were not the open and avowed enemies of Athanasius, though probably the larger number of them, either openly or covertly, held views which were in antagonism with his. The Emperor Constantius was there, giving his sanction to the proceedings. The Council confirmed the decision of the Council of Tyre with regard to the deposition of Athanasius, passed (as we have said) several canons, and formulated three creeds (or, as some writers say, four), which were cautiously and guardedly, though somewhat vaguely and indistinctly, worded, expressing to some extent views which nearly coincided with the language employed in the Nicene Creed (cf. "The Arians," iv. 3).

The Eusebians objected to the term "Homöousios" on the ground that it was applicable only to things corporeal, to men, animals, and plants, and affirmed that the term "Homœousios" was the proper one to employ of incorporeal beings, as God or angels. By such subtle distinctions the Eusebians led Constantius to adopt the Homœousion doctrine or language, through fear lest he should confound things corporeal and incorporeal; but, says Sozomen, the fear was a vain one, since, in speaking of the objects of the mind, we are constrained to derive our language from the objects of sense; and since, so long as the meaning we attach to them is correct, the mere terms are a matter of indifference (*see* Bishop Kaye, "C. of N.," 90).

All these discussions naturally occupied some considerable time, and yet no tidings of the Council had arrived at Rome. When, however, Athanasius had already spent a year and a half in that city, Julius at length assembled the long-expected Council there. It consisted of more than fifty bishops, and was held in the church of Vito, the presbyter. After the letter of the Eusebians had been read aloud, the case of Athanasius was carefully inquired into. The report of the Mareotic Commissioners, which had been brought to Rome two years before by the three envoys of the Eusebians, was laid before the Council, and the evidence of the cruelties recently inflicted by Bishop Gregory was attested by presbyters from Egypt. Gregory had himself sent as an envoy to Rome a presbyter named Carpones, who had been an associate of Arius, to soften down the reports from Alexandria, and endeavour to put a favourable construction on what had taken place there. When the Council had examined into these different allegations, and had heard the evidence on both sides, they pronounced Athanasius to be "innocent" in respect to the charges made against him, and fully recognised his right to be admitted to Church privileges and, brotherly treatment at the hands of the Bishop of Rome, which treatment he had, in fact, continued to receive from

Julius from the very first. Moreover, Marcellus of Ancyra, who, in his opposition to Arianism, had been charged with holding views which seemed, on the one hand, to trench upon Ebionism, and, on the other, on Sabellianism, and who had in consequence been deposed and expelled from his see, and had been resident at Rome for more than a year, was finally acquitted by the same Council, after having made a statement of his views, which was deemed satisfactory by the bishops of the Western Church in this Italian Council.

Different prelates and clergy were present from various places, who bore witness to injurious treatment received at the hands of the Arians. In consequence of this Julius was requested by the Council to write a synodical letter of remonstrance to the Eusebians on account of their conduct; and towards the close of the letter—which was written in the autumn of A.D. 342—he expressed his opinion that he ought to have been informed of any charges brought forward against the Bishop of Alexandria. He stated that nothing had been proved against Athanasius at the Synod of Tyre, and that the charges made against him in the Mareotis, had been made in his absence. He also announced his refusal to recognise Pistus and Gregory, adding that the bishops of Egypt, being on the spot, were more worthy of credit respecting occurrences in the Mareotis, than those who were assembled at Antioch. This letter of Julius is extant in the "Apology of Athanasius against the Arians" (§ 21–25), and is very creditable to him for the ability, resolution, and moderation which it displays.

The report that Athanasius drew up in Latin the Creed that goes by his name, while he was at Rome, and that after it had been read to Julius it was placed among the archives of the Church of Rome, and published many ages afterwards, is destitute of any shadow of proof. There is, indeed, no evidence whatever that he composed the Creed at all. He has nowhere in his writings referred to such a Creed; nor was it referred to by any writer of that and the following age; nor, indeed, heard of (says Cave) till about 600 years after the death of Athanasius; and not urged with any confidence till about 200 years after that time, when the legates of Pope Gregory IX. produced and pleaded it at Constantinople in their disputation with the Greeks. It is scarcely possible to imagine that the Creed of one so distinguished could have remained undiscovered in the archives of such a famous Church which were accessible to so many for research during so long a period.

At the commencement of the next year, 342 A.D., the Eusebian party, after having carried through their Dedication Council, endeavoured to win over to their side Constans, the youthful Emperor of the West. He had shown a kindly feeling towards Athanasius, which might have seemed strange to them, inasmuch as Constantine II. had just fallen in the civil war which had been carried on between the brothers. At the desire of Constans, Athanasius had very recently sent to him copies of the Holy Scriptures.

The Eusebians, with this motive in view, namely, that of winning over Constans to their side, sent Maris, Narcissus, and two other bishops of their party to Treves, to direct his attention to the decisions of the Councils against Athanasius, and to lay before him a Creed which appeared almost to maintain the Homöousion doctrine.

But Constans found in Maximin, the Bishop of Treves, a staunch supporter of Athanasius, and an equally firm opponent of the Eusebians—one, in fact, who would not admit these Eastern prelates into communion; and, influenced by him, Constans rejected the petition of the Eusebians, and dismissed them (Soz., iii. 10).

Athanasius, it would seem, continued to reside at Rome until the fourth year from the time of his arrival—the summer of 343 A.D.

About this time died Eusebius of Constantinople, in the height of the prosperity to which he had ingloriously attained. A twofold election followed on his death. Both Paul and Macedonius were raised to the bishopric by their respective adherents. Hermogenes, an officer of the Court, was ordered to banish Paul. The order was executed; but Hermogenes was slain.

CHAPTER XIV
Councils of Milan and Sardica

In the summer of 343 A.D., Constans wrote a letter to
Athanasius, desiring the archbishop to join him at Milan
("Ap. ad Const.," § 3, 4). He was, not unnaturally,
somewhat astonished at this command of the Emperor,
and endeavoured to discover what cause had led to it.
He found that some prelates had exerted themselves to
induce Constans to convene a fresh Council, at which
bishops both of the Eastern and Western Churches
should be present, that so, if possible, an end might be
put to the troubles of the Church.

When Athanasius reached Milan, the famous capital
of the north of Italy, he was admitted, together with
Protasius, the Bishop of Milan, to a private audience
with Constans. The Emperor received him in a very
courteous and friendly manner, and informed him that
he had sent to his brother, desiring that a Council should
be convened.

Some few years after the Council of Antioch, at
which the Eusebians had prepared three or four Creeds,
another synod met at the same place to examine into
and endeavour to settle the disputes of the Church, at

which the Eusebians made the explication or confession of faith, commonly called the "Macrostich," or the "Long Confession," to remove any suspicion of their heterodoxy that the Western Church might entertain. This Creed they presented by their delegates to the synod then sitting at Milan. In this Creed they omitted the word "Consubstantial"; asserted that the Son is "*like*" the Father, and is "true and perfect God," but "had a beginning, and was *made*, though not like other creatures" (Soc., ii. 19; Soz., iii. 11; Athan., "de Synod," § 26). To this long and prolix formula the Western bishops said briefly in reply, that they were well content with the Nicene Creed and desired no other. They evidently thought that some dangerous doctrine lurked in that long array of words. The Eusebian delegates upon this departed in indignation. In this Synod of Milan, Photinus of Sirmium—who was sometimes called "Scotinus" by a play upon his name—was condemned for his heretical views, holding, as he did, "that the Word was an energy which dwelt for a time in Christ, and that on its departure His office would come to an end." Ursacius and Valens were absolved in this synod of the charge of heresy, and admitted into communion. Towards the end of the synod, Athanasius, on the summons of the Emperor, came to Milan; but, notwithstanding his caution, he was subjected to the attacks of his enemies, who tried to poison the Emperor's mind against him.

Very soon after the interview recorded above with Constans, Athanasius quitted Milan, having been requested by the Emperor to go to Gaul that he might meet Hosius, the revered Bishop of Cordova, and accompany him to the Council, which, in accordance with the wishes of the two Emperors, was to be assembled at the city of Sardica in Mæsia, which was conveniently situated on the border-land of their respective empires, near the confines of the present Bulgaria and Servia.

About 170 bishops,[10] according to Athanasius, chiefly from the Western Church, besides the Eusebians, met together at Sardica, probably at the close of the year 343 A.D. This is the date as fixed by Hefele, though (previous to the discoveries of the Maffeian Fragment and the Festal Letters) it was usual to assign a later date—347 A.D.—for the Council. It would seem that the decision of the Council was ratified and subscribed by many bishops who were not personally present. Thus it has been alleged that the bishops of Britain were there, though this assertion—interesting as it may be to us— can scarcely be proved. Julius himself was absent from the Council through the pressure of business, but he sent two legates in his place. Hosius, who had presided at Nicæa, presided also at Sardica. The greater number of bishops assembled were clearly convinced of the innocence of Athanasius, so far as any proof to the contrary had as yet been given, and consequently rejected the decisions of the Councils of Tyre and Antioch, and joined with him in the most solemn worship of the Church.

The smaller number, however, on their arrival kept themselves confined to the lodgings in the Palace which had been assigned to them, and declined to take any part in the assembly until those in the Council whom they regarded as convicted—referring to Athanasius and his party—should be dismissed. They were informed that all

---

[10] There were present, according to Socrates (ii. 20), 300 bishops of the West and 76 of the East. This corresponds with the calculation of Sozomen (iii. 11). Theodoret (ii. 8) regards the number as 250.

points which were of a doubtful character should be discussed, and that each side should be at liberty to bring forward their objections against any member of the Council. The orthodox party had their witnesses ready to testify to the cruelties inflicted upon their brethren by the Eusebians—to give evidence of forged documents—and to exhibit the marks of wounds and bruises on their bodies inflicted by the Arianizers.

The Eusebian bishops, however, to the number of eighty, withdrew from the Council, although they were pressed with "smart provocations" to meet the charges of their opponents, and informed that, if they preferred to do so, they might be heard in private before Hosius, the presiding bishop of the Council. They saw that no force could be put on such a synod; that there were no great men present from the Court who could intimidate those who took part in it; and that Athanasius had all his proofs and witnesses at hand to confute their statements and establish his own innocence. Notwithstanding, therefore, the challenge of Athanasius to bring forward their accusations, they refused to attempt even to refute the charges of cruelty made against them; and, in opposition to the wishes of the orthodox, they constituted themselves into a Council at Philippopolis (Soc., ii. 20), which lay within the borders of the Empire of the East—though Cave thinks that all that is reported to have taken place at Philippopolis did actually take place at Sardica (114),—and at this Council reiterated the decrees against Athanasius, and, in addition, drew up others against Hosius, Julius, and other bishops; wrote a long "Encyclical Letter," giving an account of what they had done and whom they had deposed; and formulated a Creed without the word "Consubstantial," but in other respects apparently orthodox. It is worthy of remark that this Encyclical Letter put forth in their defence is one of the very few documents of the Eusebians which is extant, and may be regarded as their manifesto (as Bishop Kaye has observed, "C. of N." 98) against Athanasius and his party. It has been preserved by Hilary ("Fragm." ii. ch. 9). They repeat all the old charges against Athanasius, accusing him, in addition, of cruelty and oppression; of restoring bishops condemned by different councils; of acting in a most arbitrary and tyrannical manner on his return to Alexandria; and they conclude by urging their friends no longer to communicate with him and others whom they name, affirming that it was opposed to all ecclesiastical rule and discipline that the Churches of the West should set aside the decisions of those of the East. It would appear, from the statements of Athanasius, that the members of the Council acted with great violence after they quitted Sardica.

In the meantime the Council at Sardica prosecuted their investigations, and, as the result of their careful and deliberate inquiries, their sifting of evidence, and their examination of witnesses, pronounced Athanasius to be innocent, and restored him, with every expression of affection, to his see. They also acquitted Marcellus of Ancyra, and Asclepas of Gaza. At the same time they excommunicated eleven Eusebian bishops, who had "separated (they said) the Son from the Father, and so merited separation from the Catholic Church," and had been guilty of numberless cruelties and much evil to the orthodox. The members of the Council held firmly and exclusively to the Nicene Creed; and they wrote synodical letters of consideration and sympathy to the suffragan bishops of the Alexandrian Church, and also to all the faithful members of the Church there,

entreating them to vindicate the innocence of
Athanasius, and to strive earnestly for the true faith,
bidding them remember that those who endured unto
the end should be saved. They, moreover, published
certain canons—twenty-one in number—respecting
Church discipline, one of which provided that a
reference might be made to Julius, Bishop of Rome, so
that a bishop's case might be re-heard before him if he
desired a new trial. It could not be said that this canon
established any claim for the papal supremacy. Its
powers were too limited for such an object, and it was
probably designed to meet a mere temporary desire to
confirm the authority of Julius, and so to uphold and
maintain orthodox views. It would appear that there
were two recensions of these canons, one in Greek and
one in Latin. Such, at least, is Hefele's opinion.[11]

This outspoken opinion on the part of the Council of
Sardica not only caused very great irritation to the
Eusebian party, but also induced them to recommend
Constantius to adopt more severe and cruel measures,
not only at Hadrianople, but also in reference to the
Alexandrian Church. The magistrates of the latter city
actually received orders to behead Athanasius and
certain of his clerical followers if they came near the
city. Five of his clergy were exiled to Armenia. Many of
the orthodox were induced either to conceal their faith,
or to retreat to the desert, so that they might escape from
the ruling faction. The Council of Sardica upon hearing
this, with the assent of Constans, made an effort to
influence the conduct of Constantius by sending to him
two envoys, Euphratas the Bishop of Cologne, and
Vincentius the Bishop of Capua, who went to Antioch

---

[11] These canons are given in full in Bishop Wordsworth's "Church History,"
ii. 92, *seq.*

at the Eastertide of 344 A.D., with missives from the Council, and the letter of Constans, desiring Constantius to restore Athanasius and the other exiled bishops to their sees.

The Arian Bishop of Antioch, named Stephanus or Stephen, concocted, with the aid of Onager, a vile conspiracy against Euphratas. The plot was discovered, and Constantius (Theod., ii. 7), justly indignant at such a shameless proceeding, was moved to recall the exiled clergy from Armenia, and to send orders to check the cruelties inflicted on the followers of Athanasius. Stephen himself, who had taken the lead at Philippopolis, was deposed, and Leontius—an Arian, indeed, but of a more gentle spirit—was put in his place. Athanasius, however, who was still under the Emperor's interdict, advanced from Sardica to Naissus, a city in Dacia, and then, at the desire of Constans, to Aquileia. Not alone, but in company with Bishop Fortunatian, he had several interviews with the Emperor Constans at this city, near the walls of which Constantine II. had met with his death. We hear that Constans attended at an undedicated church in this city, and joined in the services with a large congregation, showing a respect for the outward ordinances of religion, which, together with his personal kindness, favourably influenced Athanasius's opinion of him ("Ap. to Const.").

It was currently reported that Constans urged Constantius to restore Athanasius (Soc., ii. 22), even threatening a civil war in case of his refusal.

Constantius, moved by the utter unscrupulousness of the conduct of the Eusebians, and the complete want of principle which had been displayed by Stephen, and being led to infer that he had been deceived by them, and affected probably by the bold declaration of truth made by the Council of Sardica, now completely altered his course of action towards Athanasius, and felt a strong desire for his restoration to his see.

CHAPTER XV
Athanasius's Second Restoration to His See

Gregory, who had been thrust by the civil power into the bishopric of Alexandria, so inflamed and irritated the people of Alexandria against him by his cruel atrocities, that he was slain in a popular outbreak of fury, and thus the way was cleared for the return of the lawful bishop of the see (Theod., ii. 9; Athan., "Hist. Arian.," § 21). This event occurred about February, 345 A.D. An opportunity was now afforded Constantius of giving way to the wishes of Constans. He consequently wrote to Athanasius (Soc., ii. 23), pretending to be anxious to have the sanction of Constans to this act of clemency on his part. Constantius sent in addition two other letters to Athanasius. In his second letter the Emperor offered him the use of the public carriages, and desired him to return with all speed. In his third he expressed his surprise that Athanasius had not yet returned, and sent a deacon as the bearer of a letter to him, in which he signified his earnest wish that Athanasius would make haste and come, and so be restored to his own country. Moreover, Constantius

employed six counts to write in an encouraging and
sympathetic strain to the exiled bishop.

Athanasius, when he had received these different
letters at Aquileia, resolved at last to act upon the
assurances contained in them, but would not move until
Constantius could inform Constans that he had been
waiting for a year for the return of Athanasius.
Accepting, however, an invitation to visit Constans at
Treves, Athanasius made a detour in order to see Rome
once more. Six years had now passed away since
Athanasius had been so kindly received by Julius on his
first arrival at the metropolis of the West. And now
Julius, in a letter of the greatest beauty and warmth of
feeling (Athan., "Apol.," § 52; Soc., ii. 23),
congratulates the Alexandrian Church upon the
restoration of their beloved bishop, whose many virtues
and excellences he recounts, and in whose private
friendship he rejoiced; and compliments them on the
firm faith which they had themselves displayed during
this long period of suffering and bereavement, dilating
upon the gladness with which they would welcome him
on his return; and concludes his letter with the prayer
that they might be partakers of joys which eye had not
seen nor ear heard. "If precious metals (he says), such as
gold and silver, are tried by the fire, what can be
worthily said of so great a man, who has overcome the
perils of so many afflictions, and who returns to you,
having been declared innocent, not only by us, but by
the judgment of the whole synod? Receive, therefore,
beloved brethren, with all joy, and glory to God, your
Bishop Athanasius."

Some paragraphs in this letter, especially laudatory of
Athanasius, and condemnatory of his Arian enemies
and persecutors, are contained in the copy preserved by

Socrates, but are omitted by Athanasius himself—an interesting fact, as showing both his modesty and his charity (cf. Wordsworth, "C. H.," ii. 103, note).

About the middle of the summer Athanasius went northward, had an interview with Constans, and passing through Hadrianople, where he looked upon the graves of laymen slain by Arian bishops, went on to Antioch, at which place he saw Constantius for the third time. His reception by the Emperor was a very cordial one for him, since he rarely made any display of feeling (cf. "Apol. ad Const.," § 5; "Hist. Arian.," § 22; Soc., ii. 23; Soz., iii. 20; Theod., ii. 9). Athanasius, without using any severity of language towards his opponents, expressed a wish that he might have permission to refute their statements; but Constantius, calling God to witness, solemnly assured him, that he would never again believe the charges made against him, and that all the former accusations preferred against him should be obliterated. This resolution he carried out at once, by writing, with this object in view, to the Egyptian magistrates, whom he charged to erase from the public records all orders injurious to the followers of Athanasius, and informed them that Athanasius and his adherents were to have the enjoyment of all the privileges formerly awarded to them. These instructions were carried out accordingly by the Duke and prefects of Egypt. He also sent letters in favour of Athanasius to the bishops and priests of the Egyptian Church, and also to the laity of the Catholic Church of Alexandria (Athan., "Apol.," § 54).

In consequence of this favourable action on the part of Constantius, the Bishop afterwards requested the congregation of his Church to offer up their prayers for the preservation of the most religious and gracious

Emperor Constantius.

One request the Emperor made of Athanasius, that he would permit the Arians the use of one Church in Alexandria. Athanasius immediately acceded to the request, on the condition that the Eustathians of Antioch (so named from their former bishop and confessor) might also have the use of a church for their own services (Theod., ii. 12). Constantius would have agreed to this arrangement, but his advisers (on whom he was notoriously dependent) opposed his action. From Antioch—passing on his way through Laodicea, where he was cordially received by a learned, though youthful, reader of the Church there, of the name of Apollinaris—Athanasius went on to Jerusalem. Here a Council—very different to that which had assembled there in 335 A.D.—met together to pay him respect and honour, with Maximus, Bishop of Jerusalem, at its head. They offered also their congratulations to the Egyptian Church and people by a synodical letter, on their Bishop's restoration to his see. Sixteen bishops subscribed their names to it. "We cannot (they say) sufficiently thank the Lord of all for the wonders which He works everywhere, and especially for your Church, inasmuch as He restores to you your pastor and our fellow-minister Athanasius. For who ever hoped to see those things which ye now enjoy?… Therefore, receive him with open arms" (Athan., "Apol.," § 57; "Hist. Arian. ad Mon.," § 25).

We are told by Athanasius that several bishops who had before agreed in his condemnation, abandoned their former views, and that all the Palestine bishops, with the exception of two or three, were now ready to communicate with him. We even find that his two most bitter opponents, Ursacius and Valens, sent to Julius a letter, in which they expressed their penitence, and entreated pardon for their past conduct in regard to Athanasius, confessing in the presence of their clergy that their charges against him were unfounded and calumnious, and denouncing Arianism as heretical ("Hist. Arian. ad Mon.," § 26; "Apol.," § 58; Soc., ii. 24; Soz., iii. 23). We learn that a copy of this recantation was sent by the Bishop of Treves to Athanasius. And not content with this open submission to Julius, they also sent a letter to Athanasius himself—of a less ceremonious character than the confession to Julius—in which they declared themselves to be at peace and in communion with him, and desired a like acknowledgment from him in return.

And now Athanasius once again turned his steps homeward; according to the "Festal Index," on October 21, 346 A.D., though, according to the generally-received chronology, in 349 A.D., or, according to Cave, in 350 A.D. A grand welcome awaited him. It was a splendid reception. It was a "day to make men forget the past, and to strengthen them for the future." Nor did it terminate in mere enthusiasm and excitement. "Who" (exclaims Athanasius, "Hist. Arian.," § 27) "that beheld such peace in our churches, did not wonder at the sight? Who was not gladdened by the concord of so many and great bishops? Who did not glorify God for the joy of the people in the assemblies of the Church? How many enemies repented of their hate! How many calumniators apologised for their slander! How many exchanged hatred for love! How many who had formerly been partisans of Arianism, not by conviction but by coercion, came and asked for pardon, and said that, while in bodily presence they were with the Arians, they were in heart with Athanasius!"

From the famous oration or panegyric of Gregory
Nazianzen ("Orat.," xxi. § 27, 29, 31) we learn how
imposing was the display made by his exulting church
and people. We read of a vast and thronging multitude
going forth in orderly procession to meet him, when he
was yet at some distance from the city, "like another
Nile,"—each trade, and each profession keeping its own
place,—men, women, and children apart from each
other. We hear that branches of trees were waved on
high as he approached; and that rich carpets of the
brightest colours were spread under his feet, just as
Æschylus, in his "Agamemnon," represents them as
being strewn for the king on his return from Troy. He
was all the more welcome on account of his long
absence,—"near nine years" (says Cave, p. 124) having
passed "since his last departure, and more than two full
years since his restitution by the Sardican Council,"—
and on account of the many and great calamities he had
suffered in defence of the faith, and the cruelties to
which they themselves had been exposed by their
persecutors while he was away. We read of every inch
of rising ground being covered by crowds anxious to
catch a sight of his well-known face and figure, listening
with anxious ears for the sound of his welcome voice,
while the air vibrated with the plaudits and shouts with
which he was welcomed. We are told of the
magnificence of the banquets at which he was
entertained, of the clouds of incense, and of the brilliant
illuminations which greeted his return. Never was a
bishop received with such acclamations and such
rejoicings before. "His whole course," it has been
remarked, "was that of an adventurous and wandering
prince, rather than of a persecuted theologian; and when
in the brief intervals of triumph he was enabled to return

to his native city, his entrance was like that of a sovereign rather than of a prelate."

Gregory also tells us how gracious and kindly was the bearing of Athanasius towards all his former opponents, and how earnestly he strove to unite every one in the bonds of peace and mutual affection. By such conduct on his part charity prevailed, religious feeling was deepened and strengthened, and self-devotion stimulated. We read that "the hungry and the orphans were sheltered and maintained, and every household by its devotion transformed into a church" (Theod., ii. 12).

From Antony he received an address of congratulation on his return at the hands of some monks of Tabenne, and the bearers of the address were cordially welcomed by the archbishop. Letters poured in from bishops, who assured him that, even when they sided with the Arian party, under the pressure of external compulsion, their hearts had sympathised with him. Thus, by his return, Athanasius was enabled to build up the true faith. Thus the doctrine of the blessed Trinity was once again clearly and fully preached, and, like a light shining in a dark place, was able to diffuse its glorious truths over the benighted city.

CHAPTER XVI
Life and Work at Alexandria

Athanasius was now once more among his own people in his own diocese. For six long years at least—for nine say some writers—he had been estranged from them, an exile in remote countries, and in widely separated lands. This return from his wanderings must have been a season of comparative peacefulness, rest, and satisfaction.

> *"Ecce dies celebris!*
> *Lux succedit tenebris."*
> (Adam of St. Victor).

But an event shortly occurred which appeared at first very likely to have ruined all the hopes and plans which he might have formed. The sad tidings reached him that Constans, who had ever proved a steady friend and patron to him, had been treacherously slain by rebels under Magnentius, who had usurped the title of emperor in the spring of the year 350 A.D. The loss of such a friendly protector might most justly have inspired him with the deepest alarm. By the death of Constans the whole of the Roman Empire passed into the hands of

Constantius. But his fears were to a great extent removed by the receipt of a kind message from Constantius, through Palladius the controller of the Palace, and Asterius the governor of Armenia. In this letter we find the following words of comfort:—"Because there are not wanting some, who, in this calamitous time, will be ready to terrify you with frightful rumours, we have thought good to direct these our letters to you, exhorting and commanding you, that, as becomes a bishop, you go on to instruct and build up the people in the true religion.… for that I am firmly purposed, that you shall constantly continue bishop of that see."

No wonder that his "Festal Letter," which, according to his usual custom, he composed about this time, commences with an outpouring of thankfulness that he had once more been brought in safety from far-off lands to the Church which he so much loved. At its conclusion we find an account of the installation of several bishops, and amongst them Arsenius is mentioned as being placed at Hypsale. We learn also from the same letter that several bishops of the orthodox faith were substituted in the place of Arian occupants of the sees. It would not seem improbable that, by virtue of his position at Alexandria, Athanasius claimed the right of ordination in the different dioceses of his suffragan bishops throughout Egypt. The decisions of the Council of Sardica were at this time duly accepted by the bishops in Egypt (Soc., ii. 26; Soz., iv. 1). Probably more than 400 bishops of different sees in various countries, some of them residing even in Britain, now shared communion and fellowship with Athanasius. From very many of them he had already received "Letters of Peace," to which he had now leisure to reply. Many persons who had taken the side of the Arianizers now came to him under the cover of night, offering various reasons and excuses for the step which they had unfortunately taken.

It was a season—we can scarcely doubt—of strange and unwonted quiet and repose for the bishop, which continued perhaps for nearly three years ("Hist. Arian.," § 25). The Church seemed to enjoy at length the blessing of peace; but, after all, it was in appearance rather than in reality. She had soon to learn the humiliating lesson that reliance on kings was but a poor and frail support to depend upon.

We have already seen that Valens and Ursacius— "men of unsettled principles, apt to turn as the wind blew from any quarter"—having abjured the views of Arius before a synod held at Milan, had written a letter to Athanasius, and had also expressed themselves in humble and respectful terms to Julius, Bishop of Rome, to whom they showed a greater amount of deferential respect than they did to the Bishop of Alexandria. There is, however, a degree of doubt as to the exact time when the correspondence took place, some placing it in 347 A.D., while others (as the Benedictine editor and Socrates) regarded the date as 349 A.D. Julius placed credit in their sincerity; but they afterwards—recanting their recantation—declared that it was their fear of Constans which induced them to write to him. Socrates (i. 37) says, that they always took the side of the stronger party. From the different tone of the two letters, Gibbon hesitates to affirm the genuineness of that to Julius.

(1.) At this time Athanasius found leisure to write his Letter or Treatise "On the Nicene Definition of Faith," in which, after noticing the fickleness of the Arians, their recourse to violence, their ignorant desire to set aside the decrees of a General Council, he carefully maintains the orthodox sense in which the term "Son" is employed,—defends the use of the word "Homöousion," even though it does not occur in Holy Scripture,—discusses the Arian term "Ingenerate,"—quotes authorities in defence of the Council,—and gives a clear and accurate account of the proceedings of the Nicene Council and of the protest there made against the Arians and their views. He thus concludes the Letter:—"Thou, however, beloved, on receiving this, read it to thyself; and, if thou approvest of it, read it also to the brethren who happen to be present, that they, too, on hearing it may welcome the Council's zeal for the truth and the exactness of its sense; and may condemn that of Christ's foes, the Arians, and the futile pretences which, for the sake of their irreligious heresy, they have been at the pains to frame for each other; because to God and the Father is due the glory, honour, and worship, with His co-existent Son and Word, together with the All holy and Life-giving Spirit, now and unto endless ages of ages."

(2.) He wrote also another Letter at this same time, "On the Opinions of Dionysius." which would seem, both from external and internal evidence, closely to follow the Letter to which reference has just been made (cf. the "Admonitio" in the Benedictine edition). Dionysius had been Bishop of Alexandria in the third century, and his writings against Sabellianism, about 263 A.D., had been unfairly and unjustly quoted as favouring Arianism.

(3.) He, moreover, found time to publish another work at this period of his life, namely, his "Apology against the Arians." to which he would seem to have made subsequent additions. This "Apology" is called in the Bollandist Life the "Syllogus," or collection of documents,—the documents extending from 300 to 350 A.D., of which those between 340 and 350 A.D. are placed first. Montfaucon asserts that this "Apology" is the most authentic source of the history of the Church in the first half of the fourth century. "Athanasius is far superior to any other historians of the period," it has been said, "both from his bearing for the most part a personal testimony to the facts he relates, and from his greater accuracy and use of actual documents." By these documents he trusted that the charges made against him might be satisfactorily refuted.

About this time one of the envoys sent by Magnentius to the Emperor Constantius came to Alexandria. In speaking to him respecting Constans, Athanasius is said to have wept. The bishop, not unnaturally, entertained some apprehension of what might be the line of conduct that Magnentius would adopt. He soon, however, discovered that there was more danger to be anticipated from the Arianizing party attached to Constantius than from Magnentius himself.

Thus we find that Constantius suddenly issued decrees from Arles and Milan, which were favourable to the Arians,—transferred to the Arians the portion of corn hitherto given to Athanasius,—and despatched commissioners to various magistrates and bishops, threatening them with deprivation if they did not abandon communion with Athanasius. There were some who had the courage to resist the Emperor's commands, and even dared to remonstrate with him on his injustice. Amongst them were Paulinus of Treves, Lucifer of Cagliari, Dionysius of Milan, all of whom were banished in consequence. But this severity,—so Athanasius informs us ("Ad Mon.," ch. 34),—acted disadvantageously to the Arian party,. because in his view all attempts to repress the truth by violence recoil upon the persecutors.

Once more Valens and Ursacius began to form designs against him. Accordingly, Valens pointed out to Constantius, over whom he exercised much influence, that Athanasius, if allowed to remain at peace, would lord it over them all, and would anathematise his adversaries, not excepting the Emperor himself, as being no better than concealed Manichæans, and that, therefore, on all grounds it became the Emperor to take the side of that party which was loyal and well-disposed towards him (Athan. "Ad Mon.," § 30). Influenced by such an appeal as this, Constantius at once forgot all the solemn promises which he had before made to Athanasius, all thought of the memory of Constans, and openly went over to the side of the Arians, and zealously espoused their cause.

The newly-appointed Bishop of Rome, Liberius,— the successor of Julius, who died in the spring of 352 A.D.—received a great number of letters against Athanasius, and, in addition, the offer of large presents from Constantius, together with urgent entreaties at the same time from him to condemn the Bishop of Alexandria. These overtures were made through the agency of the Eunuch Eusebius, but they were all indignantly rejected by Liberius. Rome still remained firm in its support of the Bishop of Alexandria.

Constantius was very indignant at Eusebius's want of success, and, in consequence, commenced a persecution against the orthodox, which Athanasius ("Ad Mon.," ch. 40) represents as having been more severe even than that of Maximian, inasmuch as he allowed no intercourse between those who were banished, and no enjoyment of each other's society in their sufferings, which Maximian himself had permitted. Their banishment, however, to different and distant countries, was overruled for good, inasmuch as they spread the truth wherever they went, thus acting the part of missionaries of the Gospel.

But all the Emperor's efforts failed with regard to Liberius, who not only refused to join the Arianizing party, but had the courage to rebuke Constantius for his persecution and cruelty (Theod., ii. 16, 17). In consequence of this firm and noble conduct Liberius was banished to Berœa in Thrace, and Felix appointed as his successor ("De Fugâ," ch. iv; Soc., ii. 27; Soz., iv. 11). When he was in exile, Constantius, either from compassion or from respect to his high position, sent him 500 pieces of gold; but he refused them, bidding the messenger restore them to the Emperor, who might give the money to some of his attendant courtiers, who were always craving and never satisfied. The Empress acted in a similar way, and was met by a similar refusal.

It would seem that Liberius's constancy and firmness were not proof against an exile of two years' duration, accompanied with threats of death, and that he was induced to subscribe the Creed of the Council of Sirmium, and renounce the communion of Athanasius, "whose cause" (says Fleury) "was inseparable from that of the true faith." In consequence of this concession to Constantius, Liberius was once more restored to his see.

Constantius, we may here remark, adopted a very similar plan with regard to the venerable Hosius ("Ad Mon.," § 42, 46; "De Fugâ," § 5). He earnestly solicited him to join in the condemnation of Athanasius. But he not only refused to do this, but wrote a strong letter to the Emperor, in which he contrasted the conduct of Athanasius with that of the Arian bishops at the Council of Sardica, and warned the Emperor of the account he would one day have to render for his conduct, urging him not to give his sanction to men, who, like Valens and Ursacius, after having once acknowledged the innocence of Athanasius, subsequently retracted what they had said. With men of this stamp no intercourse ought to be maintained.

Unhappily Hosius, after having been detained for a year at Sirmium, and treated so severely that it actually amounted to torture (Soc., ii. 31), weighed down by suffering and the load of 100 years, was at last induced to communicate with Ursacius and Valens, and to sign an Arian Creed, which sad concession Hilary called "Hosii deliramentum," though he still resolutely refused to affix his signature to the condemnation of Athanasius. Thus, for a time, fell one who had been a confessor in the Diocletian persecution, who had presided over the Church for sixty years, and had been president of the Council of Nicæa, and who stood in some respects the highest amongst contemporary bishops and was regarded with almost universal honour and veneration. Convinced how important it would be to attach such a man to his side, the Emperor spared no means, whether threats or flattery, to win him over. His high and noble spirit was displayed in the following reply to a peremptory letter of Constantius:—"I confessed the first time in the persecution under Maximian, your grandfather. If you likewise desire to persecute me, I am ready still to suffer anything rather than betray the truth. It is not so much a personal malice against Athanasius, as the love of heresy, which influences these men. I myself invited them to come to me and declare at the Council of Sardica what they knew against him. They dared not; they all refused.

Athanasius came afterwards to your court at Antioch: he desired his enemies might be sent for, that they might make good their accusations. Why do you still hearken to them who refused such fair proposals? How can you endure Ursacius and Valens, after they have recanted and acknowledged their calumny in writing? Remember you are a mortal man; be afraid of the day of judgment. God hath given you the empire, and hath committed the Church to our care. I write this through my concern for your eternal welfare; but with respect to your requisition, I cannot agree with Arians, nor write against Athanasius. You act for his enemies, but in the day of judgment you must defend yourself alone" (cf. Milner, "C. H." ii. 87, 88).

Permitted, after his fall, once more to return to his native country, Hosius lived to retract, earnestly protesting against the cruelty with which he had been treated, and with his dying breath entreating every one to reject the Arian heresy. He had still during his length of days much to suffer, but he was permitted, through the mercy of his God, to die in peace.

In the month of May, in the year 353 A.D., Athanasius sent five bishops (his friend Serapion being one of them) and three presbyters to Constantius to endeavour to remove some unfavourable opinions respecting him which were entertained by the Emperor. A few days after this, in the same month, Montanus, a chamberlain of the palace, reached Alexandria with an order to the Bishop not to send any envoys to the Emperor, but adding that Constantius was willing to grant Athanasius's request to visit him at Milan. As he had never made such a request, the Bishop thought that he perceived in this unsolicited permission an attempt made to draw him away from Alexandria, and replied by stating, that, as he had never made any such request, he hesitated about accepting a permission which was evidently grounded on a mistake. He should, however, be quite ready to go to Milan if the Emperor ordered him to do so. On this Montanus departed.

Shortly afterwards important tidings reached Athanasius from the seat of war. The armies of Constantius and Magnentius met in the plains of Mursa, a city of Pannonia. After a fierce engagement the army of Magnentius was entirely defeated, and he himself fled from place to place, till at length he put an end to his life in France. Constantius, not daring himself to venture into the fight, expected anxiously the issue of the battle in a Church of the Martyrs outside the city, attended only by Valens, the bishop of the place, who, by means of private intelligence, informed the anxious Emperor that his forces were victorious, pretending to have received the information from an angel, before any despatches reached the Emperor. The superstitious nature of Constantius was strongly affected by this circumstance. It not only directly increased the power which Valens and his party exerted over him, but also indirectly tended to alienate his feelings from Athanasius (Sulpic. Sever., "Hist. Eccl." ii. 38).

His victories over the Persians and Magnentius had greatly elated the Emperor, who was also puffed up by the flatteries of his courtiers of the Arian party who dared to give him the title of "Eternal," so that (as Athanasius and Hilary have remarked) those who refused to allow the eternity of the Son, had the boldness to predicate it of the Emperor.

Constantius, who had gone to spend the winter at Arles, was persuaded to hold there, instead of Aquileia, the Council which he had been requested to convene by

Liberius and many other Italian bishops. The result was unfavourable to the cause of Athanasius. The Roman legate, Vincent, joined with other bishops in condemning Athanasius; but the mantle of Maximin rested upon his successor, Paulinus of Treves, who was ready to suffer exile rather than betray the cause of the Bishop of Alexandria.

In the following Lent of the year 354 A.D. the different churches were so thronged with worshippers, that many suffered from the crush. It was, therefore, pressed upon Athanasius that he should hold the Easter Services in a large church—originally a temple erected by Hadrian, called "Hadrianeum"—which was enlarged by the Emperor, and called the "Cæsarean," but which was not yet completed, and so not dedicated. He naturally hesitated to adopt such a course, since, as it was built on royal property, to make use of it without the Emperor's consent would seem like an infringement of the authority of the State; and to employ it before dedication would be a violation of ecclesiastical discipline. He was, therefore, in doubt what course to adopt, and tried to induce the people to be content with the existing accommodation, although scanty and insufficient. The people, however, declared that they would hold the services in the open country, if the use of the Cæsarean was refused them. Under these circumstances he yielded to their remonstrance.

His Arian enemies, however, were at once ready to make this a ground of accusation against him to the Emperor. They pretended to be shocked by such a breach of ecclesiastical discipline, and at the same time they upheld the royal prerogative, which the Bishop would seem to have set aside. Athanasius dwelt on this matter in his "Apology to Constantius." He appealed to

the precedent set by his predecessor Alexander, who had
made use of the Church of Theonas before it was
completed; and to the example of the Bishops of Treves
and Aquileia, who had acted in a similar manner, in the
latter case when Constans was himself present.

This "Apology" is a very powerful piece of writing, if
you look to the force of the arguments which it contains;
it is most elegant, if you look at its wit and raillery; it is
most agreeable, if you regard the variety of the subjects
contained in it. And consequently it has been justly
placed among the best of the writings of Athanasius (cf.
"Monitum" to the "Apology" in the Benedictine
edition).

Nor was this the only ground of accusation against
Athanasius. He was also charged with having excited
Constans to act in opposition to Constantius; with
having carried on a correspondence with Magnentius;
and with not going to Italy at once when summoned by
Montanus. These were some of the charges which the
Arianizing party brought against him. In regard to the
first of these charges, Athanasius declared that he had
never conversed with Constans, except in the presence
of some other bishops. If the accusations were true,
these bishops might witness against him. He stated, in
addition, that he had never written any letter to
Constans, unless it were in defence of himself, or on
Church matters. With regard to the second charge, he
indignantly asked, whether it were likely that he should
hold any intercourse with the murderer of his
benefactor? If his enemies could produce any such
letters of his to Magnentius, let them bring them
forward.

In a short "Letter to Dracontius," which Athanasius
wrote about this time, we find him appealing with much

earnestness to his correspondent—who was a monk, and had been elected to a bishopric, but who had in fear abandoned the duties of his new position—and affectionately reminding him, not only of his religious obligations in the use of the talents intrusted to him, but also telling him that the life of a monk was not the only field for Christian self-denial. He brings forward the example of Moses, Elijah, Elisha, and the Apostles, who did not refuse to undergo the greatest struggles and conflicts in behalf of God's people. This epistle was written, according to the Benedictine editor, about the year 354 or 355 A.D.

But new troubles were in store for Athanasius. In the spring of 355 A.D., Constantius succeeded in coercing the members of a large Council, who were present to the number of 300 (Soc., ii. 36; Soz., iv. 9)—a council convened at Milan at the wish of Liberius of Rome—to join together in condemning Athanasius. It was a Council disastrous to the Church. A few only of that large assembly of bishops were faithful to the cause of Athanasius, and ready to protest against the domination of Constantius. Amongst this small number we find Lucifer of Cagliari, Eusebius of Vercellæ, Dionysius of Milan—confessors of the faith—and Maximus of Naples, who, lifting up their hands to heaven, told the Emperor that the Empire was not his, but God's, and reminded him of a Day of Judgment. He drew his sword on them in his rage, but contented himself with their banishment. Hilary, the deacon, was stripped and scourged, but he bore the indignity as a Christian, and blessed God. Maximus, after being tortured, was driven into exile, where he died; Eusebius of Vercellæ was sent into Palestine, where he suffered severely; Lucifer into Syria; and Dionysius into Cappadocia, where he shortly died. Liberius, the aged Bishop of Rome, was brought before the Emperor by his agent Eusebius the Eunuch, when he said, "Though I were single, the cause of faith would not fail: there was a time when three persons only were found who resisted a regal ordinance." He was banished, as we have seen, to Berœa, a city of Thrace.

"The controversy" (observes Dean Milman, "Hist. of Ch.," iii. 5) "became a personal question between the Emperor and his refractory subjects. The Emperor descended into the arena, and mingled in all the fury of the conflict Constantius was not content with assuming the supreme place as Emperor, or interfering in the especial province of the bishops—the theological question; he laid claim to direct inspiration. He was commissioned by a vision from Heaven to restore peace to the afflicted Church."

The designs of the Court party were directed not merely against the person, but also against the opinions of Athanasius (cf. Neander, iv. 72). The intentions of the Emperor and of the Court party against Athanasius at this time must have been manifest to every one. Constantius himself exhibited the most evident desire for his condemnation. The friends of Athanasius everywhere were subjected to the most cruel persecution. Moreover, in the summer of 355 A.D. an imperial notary, named Diogenes, took up his residence at Alexandria, and, although he abstained from seeing the bishop, and brought no letter to him, used every effort to get him expelled from the city. When Diogenes was unsuccessful in this endeavour, he quitted Alexandria in December, and then another notary named Hilarius, together with a general of the name of Syrianus, came to the city in January, 356 A.D. The Arianizers exulted in the victory which they felt was near at hand. When Syrianus was asked by Athanasius whether he was the bearer of any letter from Constantius, he said that he was not. The Bishop reminded him of the promise of safety which the Emperor had officially made to him; and the clergy and the laity also maintained with the Bishop that nothing should be done without a definite letter from the Emperor, especially as they were on the point of sending envoys to him. At this interview both the Prefect of Egypt and the Provost of Alexandria were present. At last Syrianus promised, with a solemn asseveration, that their request should be complied with. For more than three weeks after this all remained quiet; but at midnight on Thursday, February 8th, when the Bishop was engaged in a vigil-service which lasted through the night at the Church of St. Theonas, previous to the sacramental service of the next day, Syrianus the general, with 5,000 soldiers, and with Hilarius the notary, and Gorgonius the chief of the police, surrounded the church on every side. Athanasius tells us (in his "Apol. pro Fugâ," 24) that, when he heard the ill-omened uproar without, he sat down on his episcopal throne, in the depth of the choir, which was dimly lighted with lamps, and requested the deacon to read the 136th psalm, to which the people were to respond, "For His mercy endureth for ever;" and after this the congregation was to quit the Church. This solemn recitation was hardly ended before the doors of the church were violently broken open, and the brutal soldiery forced their way into the sacred building, discharging their arrows, and brandishing their swords, in the midst of the unarmed congregation, their shouts mingling with the clash of their weapons. Some of the people had already gone, but others who remained were

trampled on by the troops, matrons and virgins alike—
their ears assailed by the foulest obscenities—and some
were massacred. The seats, the holy table, the throne,
the curtains, were all alike torn from the church, and
burnt in the streets. A cry was raised for the Archbishop
to escape. This, however, he refused to do until all had
departed. He then stood up and called for prayer, and
afterwards bade all leave before him. When the majority
had left, the monks, assisted by some of the clergy,
carried him off in a swoon, resulting from the confusion
and the crush. He tells us that he passed through the
crowd of his adversaries unnoticed, by divine
interposition, and thanked God that he had secured both
his own and his people's safety ("De Fugâ," ch. 24; and
Soz., iv. 10). "He vanished,"—to use Dean Stanley's
striking words—"no one knew whither, into the
darkness of the winter night."

Athanasius then retired to a hiding-place in the
country, thankful that he had been permitted once more
to escape from the violence of his enemies, especially at
a time when his life was of the greatest consequence to
the cause of the Church in Egypt, and lay concealed "for
a little moment until the indignation should be
overpast."

No sooner had Athanasius departed than Count
Heraclius came to Alexandria with an order from the
Emperor to the Senate and people, that they should give
up the churches to the Arians, and acknowledge the
bishop whom the Emperor had sent to them. All this
was carried out with force and violence. Clergy were
treated with cruelty; virgins shamefully insulted;
Eutychius, a subdeacon, so mercilessly scourged that he
died under the infliction; no alms allowed to be given to
the poor and needy who depended on the bounty of the

Church; houses broken into and rifled; and tombs
violated in their search for Athanasius.

CHAPTER XVII
His Third Exile Spent in the Desert

When Athanasius had quitted Alexandria, he at first thought of making a personal appeal to the Emperor, who could scarcely—so he fondly imagined—have sanctioned such an outrage upon the Church. But he was deterred from taking this step when he heard the miserable tidings of what had befallen the orthodox in different quarters. Bishops of the Western Church, who had refused to stand aloof from communion with him, had either been visited with Imperial cruelty, or had been driven into exile. Many were suffering with him in that period of gloom and depression.

Nor was this all that weighed down the spirit of Athanasius. For a report reached him that, in the year 356 A.D., George, a Cappadocian (Soz., iii. 7; Greg. Naz., "Orat.," xxi.), a man of evil repute; of savage and violent temper; gluttonous, corrupt, and coarse; said to have been ordained a priest by the Arians before he was a Christian; ignorant, illiterate, and yet of worldly ability; without fear and without remorse; was on his way to Alexandria to supersede him in his bishopric; and moreover that a form of belief—vague and ill-defined, but claiming to be purely Scriptural, which set aside the Nicene Creed—was about to be put before the Bishops of Egypt for their acceptance. Epiphanius ("Hæres.," lxxvi. 1) adds that George—steeped in the vices of his native country, which was infamous for its morals—scrupled at nothing which was either violent or disgraceful, with a view to the gratification of his avarice. Many he robbed of their inheritance; he secured a monopoly of the nitre, papyrus, and salt-lakes of Egypt; he made profit even out of funerals, by only allowing the dead to be carried in biers or painted coffins of his own manufacture. And this testimony of Athanasius's supporters to the character of George is confirmed by the evidence of Ammianus Marcellinus, who speaks of his appointment to the See of Alexandria as a public calamity. And yet this man was commended by Constantius to the See of Alexandria as a "prelate above praise"—as the "wisest of teachers"—as "the fittest guide to the kingdom of heaven."

In consequence of this sad and gloomy state of things, Athanasius immediately commenced, in the emergency, an "Encyclical Letter to the Egyptian and Libyan Bishops against the Arians."

This circular Epistle was written in the beginning of 356 A.D.—though some have fixed its date at 361 A.D., forming their judgment from internal evidence— immediately after his flight in consequence of the outrages committed on the Church by Syrianus. There is not much contained in this Epistle which cannot be found in his other works. A good deal of the subject-matter is of a doctrinal character. The Arians had endeavoured to induce the Bishops to sign some of the doubtful Creeds that were then formulated. The letter was written to put them on their guard against this danger. It concludes thus: "But of these things I have no care; for I know and am persuaded that they who endure shall receive a reward from our Saviour; and that ye also, if ye endure as the Fathers did, and show yourselves examples to the people, and overthrow these strange and alien devices of impious men, shall be able to glory, and say, 'We have kept the faith;' and ye shall receive the 'crown of life,' which God 'hath promised to them that love Him.' And God grant that I also, together with you, may inherit the promises which were given, not to Paul only, but also to all them who have loved the appearing of our Lord, and Saviour, and God, and universal King, Jesus Christ."

But tidings very shortly reached him of a renewal of the same acts of sacrilege and cruelty which had taken place at Alexandria in the time of Gregory. The season of Lent was chosen, as it had been on a former occasion, for the entrance of the intruder. We hear that at Easter bishops, presbyters, virgins, widows, and the orthodox in general, were alike subjected to insult, violence, and persecution. Monasteries were burnt down—private houses were sacked—tombs were again violated in their search for Athanasius. On the Sunday after Pentecost, in the evening, at a time when the faithful had met together in a cemetery for worship apart from the Arianizers, the Duke Sebastian, an Imperial officer, and also a Manichæan, violent in temper, who sympathised with George, beset the place where they were assembled with 3,000 soldiers, and, finding some virgins and others engaged in prayer, when they refused to adopt the Arian Creed, ordered them to be scourged, and that, too, with such severity, that some died in consequence, the last rites being denied to their dead bodies.

Then followed the driving from their sees of sixteen

bishops because they declined to accept the proposed creed. Thirty more bishops were forced to take to flight; and the Desert was said to be "constantly sounding with the hymns of these pious and venerable exiles, as they passed along, loaded with chains, to the remote and savage place of their destination; many of them bearing the scars, and wounds, and mutilations, which had been inflicted upon them by their barbarous persecutors, to enforce their compliance with the Arian doctrines."

Others were intimidated into a forced assent to the creed; and the churches which had been vacated were handed over to those whose only qualification was a profession of Arian doctrines, apart from all consideration of their moral character.

Not withstanding these sad and melancholy accounts of what his diocese was suffering, Athanasius still hoped to be able to seek an interview with Constantius, until at length he heard that a letter from the Emperor had declared him to be a "runaway criminal"—a "cheat and an impostor"—who "fully deserved death;" and that in another letter the two Ethiopian kings had been urged to send Frumentius to Alexandria, in order that he might be taught by George the knowledge of God the Father, and the faith and discipline of the Church.

It was at this crisis in his career that Athanasius, feeling himself like an outcast, turned his steps to the Desert, and sought there a retreat among the many cells of the monastic fraternities. The monks and hermits were not only deeply devoted to the religious opinions of Athanasius, but also sincerely attached to his person. His rigorous austerities filled their minds with admiration. As he had proved the energetic, active, and revered bishop, so now they saw in him the mortified ascetic and the self-denying solitary. Even those who were most accustomed to bodily or mental mortification and self-sacrifice, found in Athanasius, the world-renowned patriarch of one of the most celebrated Sees in Christendom, one who equalled, if he did not outstrip, them in fasts and in devotion. Among such adherents as these he had no cause for fear. They would never betray him. He could count with perfect confidence on their good faith.

The Desert was now his home. He passed six years there in seclusion and in wandering from place to place. Still, however, he kept up, so far as he was able, a constant communication with his followers by letters. "Our Churches," so he wrote, "have been taken away from us, and given to the Arians; they have our places, and we have been banished from them. But we have the Faith: of that they cannot rob us. Which is the better of the two, the place or the Faith? Who, therefore, has lost most, or gained most? He who has the place and lost the Faith, or he who has lost the place and has the Faith? Every place is good where the Faith is. Wherever holy men dwell, the place is holy."

Athanasius was able in his own practice to reconcile both the life of the hermit and of the Cœnobite. In him it might truly be said that the active and contemplative life met.

At this time Antony died, and left his well-worn sheepskin cloak—which was the garment usually put on by the monks, and which, when it was new, Athanasius had given him—with the request that it might be returned to its donor ("Vit. Ant.," 91).

We cannot doubt that the different monastic societies would have considered their establishments highly honoured by the presence of Athanasius, an exile for the faith of Christ; and many an individual monk would have regarded his vocation ennobled by the fact that one whom he so much esteemed was sharing in their prayers, their hymns, their hours of meditation, and in their daily toil.

As it would appear that Athanasius paid furtive visits to Alexandria at this time, it is probable that he sojourned with the hermits of Lower Egypt, either those who dwelt on the Nitrian Mountain, or those who occupied that "wilderness of cells," which existed somewhat more inland; and that he only visited occasionally the monasteries of the trackless solitudes of Upper Egypt, or those of the Thebaid (Soc., iv. 23; Soz., vi. 29–31).

Romantic tales have come down to us respecting the virgin Eudæmonis, who was tortured by the Prefect, when searching at Alexandria for Athanasius; and of the young Alexandrian lady, who, according to the well-known story told by Palladius, sheltered him a few days in her house, when the pursuit after him was hot and persistent.

Athanasius's life at this period is covered with a veil of mystery and romance. Strange stories are told of his hair-breadth escapes, as he was passed on from one retreat to another, when the emissaries of the Government were closely pursuing after him. Thus we read in the life of Pachomius how a "Duke" called Artemius was following after Athanasius, and had come to a monastery named Paban, and on asking the question, "Is Athanasius here?" was answered by the leading monk Psarphi, "He is indeed the father of us all, but I have never yet seen his face." Artemius, when he found his search was vain, asked Psarphi to pray for him; but, as an Arian bishop was with him, he was met by the answer, "We may not pray with those who are in communion with Arians." Athanasius was thus handed on from monastery to monastery, and from cell to cell, sheltered from capture by those among whom he was living, with all the strange experiences in his flight and wanderings, which, in after days, might—it has been remarked—have been shared in by a Vendean or a Jacobite.

When a pause in the pursuit occurred, we find him actively engaged in correspondence with his brethren, encouraging, cheering, and advising them in their different difficulties and perplexities, and informing Serapion that the letters which he had received from his friends were of the greatest comfort to him, as proving their kindly feelings and their interest in his welfare.

Thus the "royal-hearted" exile—the "invisible patriarch"—whenever a breathing space was allowed him, was persistently occupied with the affairs of his church and diocese, keeping up the spirits of his flock, directing their energies, raising the tone of their hearts and minds, and ministering comfort and consolation to the distressed or persecuted.

He was, even in his days of retreat and concealment, like Chrysostom in the time of his exile, the centre of all the work and energy which were being displayed throughout the diocese.

> *"Great Athanasius! beaten by wild breath*
> *Of calumny, of exile, and of wrong;*
> *Thou wert familiar grown with frowning death,*
> *Looking him in the face all thy life long,*
> *Till thou and he were friends, and thou wert strong."*

(*The Cathedral.*)

CHAPTER XVIII
The Literary Harvest of His Third Exile

But during those six years of seclusion, when hiding in the midst of the caves and deserts of Egypt, we are struck with the wonderful power which Athanasius possessed of adapting himself to the circumstances under which he was placed,—a power in which he so much resembled the Apostle of the Gentiles. During that time he zealously devoted himself to literary work of different kinds, not only controversial, but also historical. He was able to pour forth from the rich stores of knowledge which he had already accumulated one work after another; for he could scarcely have obtained either any use of books to aid him, or any assistance from the living. We can picture him writing in dens and caves of the earth (for Rufinus, i. 18, recounts a marvellous story of his having spent six years in a dark and dry cistern in his concealment), or in the cells of the monks, or in some low-roofed hut, seated on a mat formed of the leaves of the palm-tree, with his roll of papyrus near him, amid the intense stillness of the desert, with no sound to break his repose, or beneath the fierce light of an Egyptian sun.[12]

(1.) At this period of seclusion, solitude, and concealment, he finished his "Apology to Constantius," a treatise upon which he had been engaged for a considerable time, and which he had hoped to have been able to deliver in person to Constantius. It may seem almost strange to observe the loyal and respectful terms in which he addresses the Emperor. He may possibly have hoped that the Emperor's tone of mind and course of conduct would improve; or he may have thought that, weak in himself, he was under the influence of stronger, but worse characters. Still, we may remark that he did not afterwards speak, as he did at this time, of the Emperor's "benignity." In this "Apology," written, according to the Benedictine editor, in 356 A.D., he both maintains his innocency, and defends himself against the various charges brought against him at different Councils and Synods; as, for example, the charge of exciting Constans against Constantius; of entering into correspondence with the tyrant Magnentius; of holding service in an unconsecrated building; of refusing to visit Constantius when invited to do so. All which charges he vigorously repelled with much force of argument, with singular wit and elegance of language, and with great abundance of facts and of detail. After what has been said of the style of Athanasius's address to the Emperor, it is strange that some authors should represent him as having written with prejudice and a strong sense of personal wrong against Constantius. If we compare what he has said of the Emperor with the language in which some of his contemporaries—notably Hilary and Lucifer of

---

[12] "The fondness" (says Dr. Bright) "of Athanasius for the illustration of the 'Light and the Ray' is well known."

Cagliari—have indulged, we shall feel disposed to marvel at the comparatively gentle tone in which he has written of the actions and motives of Constantius.

(2.) The Arians had taunted Athanasius with cowardice for his flight and concealment, and he accordingly, at this time, wrote an "Apology for his Flight," perhaps about the end of the year 357 A.D., in which he showed that his flight was justified by the will of God—the precedents afforded by good men—and the very reason of the thing. He tells us in this treatise that he regarded his flight and escape as akin to the escapes of St. Peter and St. Paul. He appealed to the examples of Jacob, and Moses, and David, and Elijah in his justification. Moreover—in addition to the conduct of different distinguished saints of God—he dwelt upon the example of Christ Himself, who avoided danger when He deemed it right to do so. He fled, so he tells us, not because he was afraid to die, but in compliance with the injunctions of Christ, that men should wait their appointed time, and not rashly tempt God; and he affirmed that he was always ready to meet death rather than renounce the faith of Christ. He spoke, also, of the persecutions, and sufferings, and violence, to which the faithful brethren were exposed, and, at the close of his "Apology," he stated by what means, through God's help, he had escaped from the church when Syrianus had beset it with his troops.

This "Apology" has always held a high place in the estimation of the writers of ecclesiastical history, who often make quotations from it in their works. This is especially the case with Theodoret, who, in the second book of his history, inserts many extracts from it.

(3.) To this same period of literary activity we may assign his "Letter to the Monks," together with the

"History of the Arians" (only in part extant, the beginning being lost), of which it formed the preface. It has been justly called a "beautiful and striking letter." The "History of the Arians," which is of considerable length, seems to furnish internal evidence—from the change of persons, the first and third being blended together, as well as from its somewhat declamatory style—of having been dictated to, and taken down by, an amanuensis. The genuineness of the work has, indeed, been doubted by some critics, who have assigned it to a companion of Athanasius. There can be no doubt that the style of the treatise is more free and lively than that of his other works.

It is quite possible that he wrote this epistle to the "Ascetics that were in all places leading a monastic life," to gratify those among whom he was now tarrying. In it he narrated the calamities in which the Church was involved; the corrupt and wicked practices of the Arians; and the sufferings of the orthodox in defence of the Catholic faith. The letter was, in all probability, written in the year 358 A.D.

(4.) Then followed, in the same year, his brief "Letter to Serapion," who was Bishop of Thmuis, and a friend of Antony the Monk. In it he gives, at the request of Serapion, an account of the death of Arius, the particulars of which he had obtained from Macarius, his presbyter, an eye-witness of the scene. Neander (iv. 58) censures Athanasius for attributing to Arius an intention of deceiving Constantine as to his views. It is, however, difficult to imagine, from a consideration of the whole account, that he did not intend to impose upon Constantine's credulity.

(5.) At this time were written the four great and important "Orations," or "Discourses Against the

Arians," which the learned Montfaucon (the writer of Athanasius's Life in the Benedictine edition) has declared to be "the sources whence arguments have been borrowed by all who have since written in behalf of the Divinity of the Word."

It is quite possible that modern readers may characterise portions of his arguments as somewhat overstrained and as not quite applicable to the purpose in hand; and that the severe, logical reasoning which Erasmus and other writers have attributed to Athanasius is sometimes overlaid by the declamatory style of oratory which is engendered by religious controversy; yet the fulness and richness of Scriptural illustration found in them must be acknowledged by all unprejudiced readers, as well as the firm hold which he takes of the true and divine Sonship of Christ. Moreover, we cannot but observe his keen detection of Arian fallacies, and his masterly analysis of them, as well as his passing exposure of earlier forms of heresy, such, for example, as those of Paul of Samosata, of the Manichæans, and of the Gnostics; and not only so, but his anticipatory refutations of errors yet to be, such as those of Nestorius and Eutyches. And, once more, he shows, with intense earnestness of purpose, how the orthodox form of belief is able to minister to the deepest needs and longings by which the soul of the believer is affected.

It has been proved by convincing arguments by the annotator of the Benedictine edition, that the number of these orations was four, not five, as some writers have supposed, and that the "Encyclical Letter to the Bishops of Egypt and Libya" is entirely distinct from these discourses.

The four treatises form (so it is generally thought)

one closely-connected and united whole—"une seule pièce," as Tillemont expresses it—though it must be acknowledged that some critics have regarded the 4th, not so much a continuous discussion, as a collection of fragments or memoranda—a view strongly advocated by the. editor of these treatises in the "Library of the Fathers."

Photius dwells on the fact that these orations were written in a clear and simple, but not diffuse, style, and affirms that though Athanasius employs a logical method, yet that he does it philosophically and discreetly, without being a mere slave to the terms which he makes use of, or being led away, like a youthful novice in the art, by the desire of self-display.

(1.) The first discourse treats of the deep importance of the subject-matter under discussion. It affirms that Arians are not Christians, since they follow Arius instead of Christ; that it is useless to appeal to Scripture when the doctrine is heretical; that Arianism is in fact Atheism; that Arius's "Thalia" excites horror; and that the doctrines of Arius differ widely from those of the orthodox. It brings forward evidences from Scripture and from reason of the eternity and uncreatedness of the Son; and it discusses various objections against the orthodox doctrines, and contains comments on passages of Scripture, which the Arians alleged to be favourable to their views; as, *e.g.*, Phil. 2:9, 10; Ps. 45:7, 8; and Heb. 1:4.

Speaking of the cause which induced him to write these discussions, Athanasius remarks:—"Whereas one heresy and that the last, which has now risen as harbinger of Antichrist, the Arian, as it is called, considering that other heresies, her elder sisters, have been openly proscribed, in her cunning and profligacy, affects to array herself in Scripture language, like her father the devil, and is forcing her way back into the Church's paradise—that with the pretence of Christianity, her smooth sophistry (for reason she has none) may deceive men into wrong thoughts of Christ—nay, since she has already seduced certain of the foolish, not only to corrupt their ears, but even to take and eat with Eve, till in their ignorance which ensues they think bitter sweet, and admire this loathsome heresy; on this account I have thought it necessary, at your request, to unrip 'the folds of its breastplate,' and to show the ill-savour of its folly. So while those who are far from it may continue to shun it, those whom it has deceived may repent; and, opening the eyes of their heart, may understand that darkness is not light, nor falsehood truth, nor Arianism good; nay, that those who call these men Christians are in great and grievous error, as neither having studied Scripture, nor understanding Christianity at all, and the faith which it contains."

(2.) The second discourse, which followed at some interval after the first, pursues a similar kind of argument, and refers especially and with great fulness to a text very frequently adduced by the Arians, Prov. 8:22 (in the LXX version), after having before explained Heb. 3:2, and the sense of the term "made."

Speaking of Scripture illustrations as enforcing the true doctrine, though imperfect in themselves, Athanasius writes:—"Such illustrations and such images has Scripture proposed, that, considering the inability of human nature to comprehend God, we might be able to form ideas even from these, however poorly and dimly, as far as is attainable. And as the Creation contains abundant matter for the knowledge of the being of a God and a Providence ('for by the greatness and beauty of the creatures proportionably the Maker of them is seen,' Wisd. 13:5), and we learn from them without asking for voices, but hearing the Scripture we believe, and surveying the very order and the harmony of all things, we acknowledge that He is Maker and Lord and God of all, and apprehend His marvellous providence and governance over all things; so in like manner about the Son's Godhead, what has been above said is sufficient, and it becomes superfluous, or rather it is very mad to dispute about it, or to ask in an heretical way, How can the Son be from eternity? or, How can He be from the Father's substance, yet not apart? since what is said to be of another is a part of Him; and what is divided is not whole. These are the evil sophistries of the heterodox; yet, though we have already shown their shallowness, the exact sense of these passages themselves and the force of these illustrations will serve to show the baseless nature of their loathsome tenet. For we see that reason is ever, and is from him and proper to his substance, whose reason it is, and doth not admit a before and an after. So again we see that the radiance from the Son is proper to it, and the Son's substance is not divided or impaired; but its substance is whole and its radiance perfect and whole, yet without impairing the substance of light, but as a true offspring from it. We understand in like manner that the Son is begotten not from without but from the Father, and while the Father remains whole, the Expression of His Subsistence is ever, and preserves the Father's likeness and unvarying Image, so that He who sees Him, sees in Him the Subsistence too, of which He is the Expression. And from the operation of the Expression we understand the true Godhead of the Subsistence, as the Saviour Himself teaches when He says, 'The Father who dwelleth in Me,

He doeth the works which I do'; and 'I and the Father
are One,' and 'I in the Father and the Father in Me.' "

(3.) The third discourse gives the interpretation of
certain texts in the Gospels (such, *e.g.*, as John 14:10;
17:3, 11; 10:30; 3:35; Mat 28:18; Mark 13:32; Luke 2:52;
Mat. 26:39; John 12:27, &c.), and exhibits Christ as
combining in Himself true Godhead and true Manhood.
It begins by noticing the doctrine of the Coinherence,
and then passes on to the consideration of another Arian
assertion, that "the Sonship was the result of God's
mere will."

We quote one passage from the third discourse on
the right mode of interpreting Scripture.

"Now, what has been briefly said above may suffice
to show their misunderstanding of the passages they
then alleged; and that of what they now allege from the
Gospels they certainly give an unsound interpretation,
we may easily see, if we now consider the drift of that
faith which we Christians hold, and using it as a rule
[the "Regula Fidei,"] apply ourselves, as the Apostle
teaches, to the reading of inspired Scripture. For Christ's
enemies, being ignorant of this drift, have wandered
from the way of truth, and have stumbled on a stone of
stumbling, thinking otherwise than they should think.
Now, the drift and character of Holy Scripture, as we
have often said, is this, it contains a double account of
the Saviour; that He was ever God, and is the Son, being
the Father's Word and Radiance and Wisdom; and that
afterwards for us He took flesh of a virgin, Mary,
Mother of God, and was made man. And this scope is
to be found throughout inspired Scripture, as the Lord
Himself has said, "Search the Scriptures, for they are
they which testify of Me."

(4.) The fourth discourse is, according to the critic

already referred to, an unarranged collection of memoranda, or heads of argument, directed against the heresies which were ascribed to his friend Marcellus and his followers, and which Athanasius himself, about 360 A.D., seemed compelled to allow a not wholly unmerited imputation, though he scarcely liked to take an active part in opposing him, from a tender feeling towards an old and beloved companion. There is, no doubt, a strong contrast between the vigorous language in which Athanasius denounces Arius, and his gentler style towards a former associate. Nor is this strange. He may secretly have been prepared to believe that Marcellus had actually passed into heresy. But with regard to Arianism, he entertained no such doubts. He deeply realised all the evil conclusions to which the opinions of Arius tended. He believed that the Arians were (so far as their tenets were concerned) the "enemies of Christ," and he employed strong language in order to warn others respecting them. And, moreover—as Dr. Bright has remarked—the language of controversy in the fourth century was not of that bland and calmly-dispassionate character which many affect in the present day. Truth was then felt to be vital, and error was felt to be deadly. Regarding the views of the Arians—in their plain and unvarnished meaning—to be not only heterodox, but as leading to apostasy from Christ, he did not dare to soften his language, or conceal what he thought to be the direct result of such teaching as theirs. He felt, too, that for thirty years the Arians had done all they could to ruin him and his cause, and the cause of Christ's Church at the same time. He was conscious that against him personally their envenomed shafts were chiefly aimed; that the persecution was principally directed against his own life; and that at sixty years of age he had now to live the life of an outlaw, expelled from the "evangelical throne," and to end his days of wandering and concealment in some cell, away from the society of his most cherished friends. But still—though the outlook was gloomy—he did not yield to despondency. He felt assured that the cause for which he had so long striven, and for which he was still striving, would in the end prevail. His faith was firm on this point. He bore up manfully, cheered by the letters which ever and anon he received from his friends. In all the present gloom and darkness he could see light at the last.

This fourth discourse treats also of the "Monarchia," which clearly implies the substantial existence of the Word and Son. In it are explained several texts against the Arians, viz., Matt, 28:18; Phil. 2:9; Eph. 1:20. A comparison is instituted between the Photinians and the Arians, who both imply that "the Word was, not indeed created, but developed to create us"; the Sabellian doctrine is shown "to preclude all real distinctions of personality in the Divine Nature"; and the identity of the Word with the Son is argued and asserted against both Photinians and Samosatenes.

We would quote one passage in the fourth discourse relating to Sabellianism. Athanasius's words are:—"If, then, Arius raves in saying that the Son is from nothing, and that once He was not, Sabellius raves also in saying that the Father is Son, and again, the Son Father, in subsistence One, in name Two; and he raves also in using as an example the grace of the Spirit. For he says, "As there are diversities of gifts, but the same Spirit, so also the Father is the same, but is dilated into Son and Spirit." Now this is utterly extravagant; for if as with the Spirit, so it is with God, the Father will be the Word and Holy Spirit, to one becoming Father, to another Son, to another Spirit, accommodating Himself to the need of each, and in name, indeed, Son and Spirit, but in reality Father only; having a beginning in that He becomes a Son, and then ceasing to be called Father, and made man in name, but in truth not even coming among us; and untrue in saying 'I and the Father,' but in reality being Himself the Father, and the other extravagances which result in the instance of Sabellius. And the name of the Son and Spirit will necessarily cease, when the need has been supplied; and what happens will altogether be but make-belief, because they have been displayed, not in truth but in name. And, the name of Son ceasing, as they hold, then the grace of Baptism will cease, too; for it was given in the Son. Nay, what will follow but the annihilation of the Creation? (See "Library of the Fathers," St. Athanasius.)

(5.) While still in concealment in the desert, Athanasius followed up these "Discourses against the Arians" by four "Letters to Serapion," Bishop of Thmuis, his beloved friend, in which letters, while the second recapitulates what had been said in the discourses; the other three dwell upon an erroneous view which was germinating (so he learnt from Serapion) at that time, and which afterwards developed into Macedonianism, which, abandoning the false teaching of the Arians respecting the Son, endeavoured to establish a similar heresy in regard to the Holy Spirit, whom the Macedonians regarded not as a Divine Person, nor even a Divine Attribute, but as a ministering creature, scarcely differing, except in degree, from the angels. Athanasius, however, contended earnestly for a real and undivided Trinity, in which the Spirit was included as well as the Father and the Son, and vigorously replied to the objections which were directed against the Spirit's co-equal personality.

CHAPTER XIX
His Third Restoration to His See

Immediately on his return to his see, in 362 A.D., Athanasius determined to convene a council at Alexandria to decide—in conjunction with Eusebius of Vercellæ, near Turin, in Cisalpine Gaul, and Eustathius of Antioch, and many Egyptian bishops—upon several very urgent matters.

In the first place, many of the bishops, who had yielded to pressure and signed the creed of Ariminum, now repented of what they had done, and desired to renounce the step which they had taken. In the next place, it was very necessary to decide how Paulinus and his followers were to act at Antioch, now that the restoration of Meletius had exaggerated the already existing difficulty. Euzoius, from his high estimation of Paulinus, had permitted him to perform service in a small church in the "New Town," while Meletius occupied the Apostle's Church in the "Old Town," near the banks of the river Orontes. In the third place, a controversy had sprung up between the orthodox as to the word "hypostasis"—a word of various meanings, but which Athanasius had used in the Nicene Council in the sense of "essence" (cf. Heb. 1:3), though apparently ("Orat.," iv. 25, 35) he used it on rare occasions in the sense of "personality," its primary idea being, according to etymologists, the "sediment of a liquid." No small number of orthodox believers at this time, especially those who had come out of semi-Arianism, were accustomed to speak of "*three* hypostases" in the Godhead, though the majority of the orthodox held to the older expression, "*one* hypostasis." In consequence of this vagueness of meaning, the advocates of the latter sense charged the advocates of the former with Arianizing, while the former charged the latter with Sabellianizing. Could not steps be taken, by means of a council, to avoid this state of things? And again, in the fourth place, there were some who seemed to lower the Incarnation to "an association between the Word and a saintly human individual," thus foreshadowing the Nestorian error. Already had Athanasius been very careful to avoid all idea of a merely moral union between the Father and the Son, by which the latter would be lowered to a saintly standard. There were, however, others who were inclined to lower the human element in the mysterious union, excluding from the manhood of Christ the reasonable soul.

The work, therefore, of the council would be a work of reconciliation—an attempt to harmonise the different views held by those who were orthodox, and reduce them to one standard. For such a work as this Athanasius, in the judgment of Gregory Nazianzen, was admirably fitted. Moreover, it was a work which would be eminently congenial to the disposition and qualifications of the excellent Eusebius of Vercellæ, who was returning home to his diocese after suffering banishment in the Thebaid, and whose presence at

Alexandria at this juncture may have been one of the chief reasons for convening the synod. Lucifer of Caliaris, who had been Eusebius's companion in exile—a man of severe and stern views, and of great impetuosity of character—had left him and gone on to Antioch.

The Council generously resolved that, in the first place, any one who had lost the privilege of Church membership might be restored upon his simple profession of the Nicene Creed, and his condemnation of the prevailing heresies of the day. At a later period Athanasius would seem to have excused the Ariminian bishops on the principle of "economy," though he apparently uses the phrase in an unobjectionable sense as meaning (so it has been said) "the considerateness which, without compromise of truth, will adapt teaching to the recipient's capacity." And secondly, in regard to the state of the Church at Antioch, it resolved that, on such terms as those stated above, the congregation of Meletians in the "Old Town" might be joined to the other community of Paulinus in the "New Town," who were considered to represent the old "Eustathians." Thirdly, with regard to the theological questions raised, it was discovered that they might be reconciled without any sacrifice of truth. It was found that the differences, when investigated, were rather verbal than real; that when, for example, *three* hypostases were spoken of, it was understood to mean three "really existing *persons*," and when *one* hypostasis was asserted, it was intended to convey the idea of one "*essence*." It was, therefore, proposed that the language of the Nicene Creed should be employed by both parties.[13] Moreover, fourthly, it

---

[13] The Nicene anathemas clearly implied *one* hypostasis. Meletius and his party spoke of *three*, while Paulinus and the Latins spoke of *one*. Jerome

appeared on examination that there was no inclination to reject either the actual Incarnation of the Word, or the completeness of the manhood which He assumed. The Council also affirmed the consubstantial divinity of the Person of the Holy Ghost.

The proceedings of the Synod were carried out with such a spirit of wisdom and with so much conciliation, that they even secured the approval of Gibbon (ch. xxiii.).

An interesting and high-toned "Synodal Letter," which has been described as "a noble monument of pacific moderation and of candid and comprehensive unity," was composed by Athanasius, on the request of the Council, and addressed to the inhabitants of Antioch. But it unfortunately arrived too late to establish the peace and concord which it was designed to effect. For the impetuous Lucifer, not waiting for the decision of the Council, had taken upon himself the responsibility of consecrating Paulinus as the lawful bishop of Antioch, and so the division still remained, which the wiser and more prudent bishops at the Council had hoped to have seen healed. Nor was this all; for his passionate indignation against the "Ariminians" had led him to form a schism of his own, rather than allow of their re-entering into Church communion, except as lay penitents. We cannot doubt that the conduct of Lucifer must have proved a source of severe disappointment and grief to Athanasius, who had regarded him with much esteem, and viewed him in the light of a confessor for the faith of Christ. Lucifer, no

---

seems to have regarded the phrase "Three hypostases" as untenable, deeming it Tritheistic. Socrates (iii. 7) mistook the line taken by the Council, thinking that it proscribed the words "Ousia" and "Hypostasis." Didymus, who had worked under Athanasius, employed the term "Hypostases" for "Persons."

doubt, manifested great contempt for the world and zeal against the Arians. He warmly defended the cause of Athanasius both in synods and before kings, and was in consequence exiled first to Germanicia in Syria, and then to Eleutheropolis in Palestine. It was at the latter place that he wrote his first book against Constantius, which he had the boldness to send to the Emperor, and to acknowledge that he was the author of the work to Florentius, the master of the imperial palace. In it he bids the Emperor not to meddle with matters ecclesiastical, and compares him with the worst of tyrants. In his second book against Constantius he advocates the cause of Athanasius in a way that approved itself to Jerome and some other fathers. His language, however, in addressing Constantius, was in the highest degree disrespectful. In consequence of these writings he was banished to the Thebaid, where he remained till the Emperor's death. In addition, however, to the schism to which we have above alluded, he was, unhappily, guilty of another. In the Council of Alexandria Athanasius had permitted the bishops who had been guilty of defection at the Council of Ariminum to retain their bishoprics on the assurance of their repentance; but Lucifer refused to communicate either with the penitent prelates, or with those who received them, and many joined with him in this schism in various parts of the world. Lucifer lived for nine years after his return to Caliaris, and resolutely maintained his schismatical principles to the end of his life.

The heathen at Alexandria had been censured by Julian for their murder of Bishop George. He listened, however, only too readily to their complaints against Athanasius, as one who by his influence might prove a dangerous opponent to paganism. He informed them that it was not with his sanction that Athanasius had resumed his episcopal office at Alexandria; and he gave a decisive order that he should quit the city. He also sent another letter to the prefect, Ecdicius by name (cf. Theod., iii. 3; Soc., ii. 13, 14; Soz., v. 15), in which he spoke of Athanasius as the "foe of the gods," as a "meddler," a "miscreant," a "paltry manikin," and as one who had ventured, in his reign, to baptize Greek ladies, referring to some conversions from paganism which he had brought about since his return. He threatened, also, to adopt severer measures towards him. This edict of the Emperor was conveyed to the bishop by a heathen philosopher of the name of Pythiodorus on the 23rd of October. His faithful brethren surrounded him, and shed tears at the cruel order. But he assured them that it was but a passing cloud, and that the darkness would soon be gone.

And now commenced his fourth exile (Soz., iii. 14 Theod., iii. 5).

CHAPTER XX
His Fourth Exile by The Banks of the Nile

Athanasius immediately went on board a boat to ascend the Nile. But Julian's orders were not neglected. A government vessel pursued the one that conveyed the bishop. Its crew inquired of a boat which they saw coming down the river where Athanasius was? The reply was that "he was not far off." The boat was in fact his own, for the bishop had ordered the sailors to tack about in order to show them that "our protector is more powerful than our persecutor;" and, it may be, he himself was the speaker (Theod., iii. 9). He had received information of his danger through some of the various channels which were open to him, and by his presence of mind he had escaped the peril. He himself sailed on in the direction of Alexandria, but hid himself at Chærea, the first station from the city. He afterwards proceeded to Memphis, where he wrote his "Festal Letter" for 363 A.D., and subsequently made his way to the Thebaid and to Thebes. He despatched this "Festal Letter" to all the country, while he himself was driven by persecution from Memphis to Thebes.

It was probably about this time, a little before Easter,

in the year 363 A.D., that Theodore of Tabenne met
Athanasius as he was drawing near to Hermopolis.
Observing the banks of the river to be crowded with
bishops, clergy, and monks, Athanasius exclaimed, in
the words of Isaiah, "Who are these that fly as a cloud,
and as doves to their cotes?" The demonstration took
place under cover of night. Athanasius quitted his boat,
and mounted on an ass, which Theodore led, and so
made his way through a vast throng of monks, who bore
lanterns and torches, and sang psalms. The archbishop
cried out on seeing them, "It is not we that are fathers, it
is these men, devoted to humility and obedience;—
blessed, indeed, and worthy of all praise are these men
who always carry the Lord's Cross;—'quorum
ignominia vere est gloria, quorum labor vere requies.' "
He tarried some time at Hermopolis and Arsinoe in
order to preach there, and then went southward to
Tabenne, noticing every thing on his way, even down to
the seats on which the monks sat, and speaking in high
terms of praise of the abbot. When Theodore and the
monks begged to be remembered in his prayers, the
archbishop characteristically replied—"If I forget thee,
O Jerusalem!"

We learn from another account that Athanasius
being at Arsinoe at midsummer, and terrified at the idea
of being taken captive and put to death, Theodore and
another abbot of the name of Pammon, came to visit
him, and observing his alarm, persuaded him to embark
with them on Theodore's closely-covered boat, that he
might go and hide himself away at Tabenne. The wind
being against them, Theodore's monks began to tow the
boat. Meantime, Athanasius was engaged in prayer,
with the idea of a martyr's death before him. He began
to address the two abbots with an expression of fear that

he might be called upon to endure a violent death, when they smiled at each other, and Theodore—so runs the tale—assured him that there was nothing for him to fear, since Julian had just been slain in the Persian war in which he was then engaged. The Emperor's death took place on June 26th, 363 A.D. Julian's sole empire only lasted for the short space of one year and not quite nine months, when he received his fatal wound, which led him to exclaim, "Thou hast conquered, O Galilean!" He died, "perhaps happily for his fame." It has been remarked by Dean Milman ("H. of C." iii. vi.),—"He might have arrested the fall of the empire, but that of paganism was beyond the power of man. His attempt to restore paganism was like that of Rienzi to restore the liberties of Rome. Julian could not have subdued Christianity, without depopulating the empire, nor contested with it the sovereignty of the world, without danger to himself and to the civil authority; nor yielded, without the disgrace and bitterness of failure."

Thus the cloud had passed away, as Athanasius had expressed the hope that it would do, when he addressed his faithful brethren on leaving Alexandria.

During this present brief period of exile Athanasius wandered through a region and through cities which have called forth the deepest interest in men of every class—literary, scientific, and religious. And if, as we have already seen, he was disposed to inspect, with the closest scrutiny and attention, the cells of the monks, the internal arrangement of their dwellings, and even the seats on which they sat; if this be so, it is scarcely possible to conceive that, with his inquisitive and thoughtful mind, he did not view with equally eager interest the old capital of Egypt with all its varied associations, or that he could have been indifferent to

the attractions of storied Thebes, or of such cities as
Arsinoe and Hermopolis. Well read, as he undoubtedly
was, in the history and archæology of Egypt, Memphis,
the Noph of the Old Testament,—the ancient capital of
the entire kingdom of Egypt, whose foundation was
traced back to Menes, the "first mortal king" of the land;
a city which would appear to have had a circuit of at
least fifteen miles, and which was old even in the time of
Herodotus—Memphis would not have failed to possess
an attraction for him which he could not have resisted.
It was famous, too, for the healthfulness of its climate,
the richness and fertility of its soil, and the beauty of its
surrounding scenery. Its bright green meadows, its
wealth of roses, its magnificent trees of vast girth and
size claimed the favourable notice both of Roman and
Grecian writers. Athanasius would have seen there not
only these physical beauties, but would also have been
attracted by the numerous temples which abounded in
the city. There he could have traced the worship of Apis,
of Isis, of the sun, of Serapis, of ancient Ptah or
Hephæstos, of all which he had heard and read much in
his studies at Alexandria.

And when he visited Thebes—the No-Ammon of the
Jewish Scriptures—he would have found equal food for
his mind and imagination to dwell upon. As old,
perhaps, as Memphis itself, girt in by the Arabian and
Libyan chain of mountains, with a site equal in size to
that of ancient Rome, it was covered with temples and
sphinxes, with the monuments of the dead and with
royal sepulchres. In its lofty houses a vast population
was concentrated. Old Homer had sung of its hundred
gates and its 20,000 war-chariots. Its palmy days were
between 1600 and 800 B.C.—long ages before the time
of Athanasius. The monuments that now remain

forcibly remind us of its ancient grandeur and beauty.
Luxor and Karnak declare what it once was. To
Athanasius the sight of that old-world city must have
borne a sad evidence of departed greatness and
magnificence. But as he wandered—as he probably
did—amongst its temples, and vast necropolis, and
broken columns and obelisks, he must have been struck
with the changes and chances of this world, and must
have felt that the only changeless object on which the
mind of man could dwell, was the great and infinite
God whom he served and worshipped. Or when he
preached at Arsinoe, he could not fail to call to mind
Ptolemy Philadelphus of Alexandrian celebrity, who
had erected the city in honour of his favourite sister
Arsinoe—a city which, from its advantageous position,
had drawn to itself much traffic and commerce; or when
at Hermopolis, with the same object of preaching the
Gospel, he found a city which not only abounded in
wealth, but was also a place of great resort, where the
hand of the Ptolemies might again be traced in the
magnificent architecture of the temples of Typhôn and
Thoth, the latter being identical with the Greek Hermes,
the inventor of letters and of the art of writing.

Such were the scenes amidst which Athanasius
wandered during this period of exile, nor can we
suppose that his well-stored mind, conversant alike with
Egyptian and classical literature, could have been
indifferent to the varied objects which he saw all around
him. The monks and their monasteries, the hermits and
their cells, no doubt filled his mind with deep thoughts
of the religious life, of the littleness of the pomps and
glories of this world, of the greatness of eternity, of self-
sacrifice and self-endurance; but he could not close his
eyes to the vast receptacles of the dead that rose in

solemn, silent grandeur around him; to the magnificent
temples which Egyptian piety had reared to its many
and strange gods; to the dim and distant antiquity of the
human race, with a civilisation and culture reaching
back long centuries before his day; to what Egypt was
when Rome, and Greece, and the Jewish nation were
each alike unknown. High thoughts must have filled his
mind as his eye gazed upon those relics of the mighty
dead. And, as he mused,

*In all its glory flowed along The old majestic river, as it had
flowed in days when Moses and the children of Israel stood
beside its banks, as he then stood and delivered his message of
reconciliation to men whose hearts beat in sympathy with his
own.*

CHAPTER XXI
His Fourth Restoration to His See

Athanasius now returned once again to Alexandria, but he did not do so openly. He entered the city by night, and remained in concealment. But he presently received a most laudatory letter from Jovian, the successor of Julian, entreating him to return and resume his functions at Alexandria, and not only so, but also to embody in writing his idea of the orthodox faith.

Athanasius accordingly convened a Council, and framed—so it has been supposed—a "Synodal Letter" (Theod., iii. 3), in which he included the Nicene Creed; showed that it was in agreement with the language of Scripture; and pointed out that the large majority of the Churches (including the British) advocated it. Moreover, he condemned Arianism; he demonstrated the inadequacy of the semi-Arian theory; he affirmed that the "Homöousion" was expressive of the real Son-ship of the Word; and he maintained the co-equality of the Holy Ghost in language which was partially anticipative of the statements of the Council of Constantinople.

On September 5th Athanasius sailed for Antioch, the bearer of this Synodal Letter. He met with a most gracious reception at Court, the rival Bishop Lucius having been treated with coldness and impatience by Jovian, who, nevertheless, during his short reign, showed himself to be not only orthodox, but also tolerant. The emissaries of the Arians from Alexandria endeavoured to depreciate and traduce Athanasius, and made several appeals to the Emperor against him, but he resolutely stood his ground in favour of Athanasius; and when at last they said that he spoke well enough, but dissembled in his heart, the Emperor replied that it was enough that he spoke well and preached truly, and that if with his tongue he taught aright, but believed amiss in his heart, in that case he was answerable only to God, for we can only hear what is spoken, while God alone knows what is in the heart.

The prospects of the Christian Church must at this time have seemed brighter to Athanasius than they had done since 330 A.D. Liberius of Rome made an explicit confession of his orthodoxy; and many bishops of the Western Church had—in response to the appeals of Eusebius and Hilary of Poitiers—renounced the Ariminian Creed and adopted the Nicene. Troubles, indeed, still existed in the ill-fated city of Antioch. At first Athanasius felt disposed to recognise Meletius, but he being greatly annoyed by the consecration of Paulinus by Lucifer—although Athanasius had had nothing whatever to do with that act—stood apart from the offers of the Bishop of Alexandria, and put him off with promises of an indefinite nature. Such being the case, Athanasius now recognised Paulinus as the true head of the Church of Antioch, and maintained the affection which he had felt for the Eustathians ever since he had worshipped with them in 346 A.D. Paulinus signed, at the wish of Athanasius, a declaration of his orthodoxy, which (so Epiphanius thinks, "Hæres." lxxvii. 20) Athanasius had probably himself framed.

He wrote his "Festal Letter" for 364 A.D. at Antioch, and after that Athanasius reached Alexandria a few days before Jovian's sudden and unexpected death. His successor was Valentinian I., who soon afterwards assigned the East to his brother Valens. Both were sincere in their profession of Christianity, but Valentinian advocated the "Homöousion" Creed, while Valens, who had been baptized by Eudoxius, was not only an Arian, but also persecuted those whose views were at variance with his own. Both Valentinian and Valens carried on a prosecution against magic and unlawful divination, in which much severity was employed.

At first it would seem that the Church of Alexandria was not injuriously affected by this change of rulers.

It is probable that in 364 or 365 A.D. Athanasius published his "Life of Antony," which he addressed "to the monks abroad" meaning by that the monks of Italy and Gaul. This Life has come down to us. "Some critics, indeed (observes the author of 'Historical Sketches' vol. iii. 97), doubt its genuineness, or consider it interpolated. Rivetus and others reject it; Du Pin decides, on the whole, that it is Athanasius's, but with additions; the Benedictines and Tillemont ascribe it to him unhesitatingly. I conceive (he adds) no question can be raised with justice about its *substantial* integrity; and on rising from the perusal of it, all candid readers will pronounce Antony a wonderful man. Enthusiastic he certainly must be accounted, according to English views of things." It was said that two young officers found in a cottage where some monks lived, a copy of the Life, which so affected them, that they resolved to give up their secular calling, and devote themselves as monks to the service of God. We know, too, that the Life of Antony had its influence in the conversion of St. Augustine.

Antony (as we learn from the author above quoted) was born A.D. 251, while Origen was still alive, while Cyprian was Bishop of Carthage, Dionysius was Bishop of Alexandria, and Gregory Thaumaturgus of Neocæsarea. He lived till A.D. 356, to the age of 105, when Athanasius was battling with the Emperor Constantius, nine years after the birth of St. Chrysostom, and two years after that of St. Augustine. He was an Egyptian by birth, and the son of noble, opulent, and Christian parents. He was brought up as a Christian, and, from his boyhood, showed a strong disposition towards a solitary life. Before he arrived at man's estate he had lost both his parents, and was left with a sister, who was a child, and an ample inheritance. His mind at this time was earnestly set upon imitating the Apostles and their converts, who gave up their possessions and followed Christ.

But Athanasius was not long free from anxiety and trial. Probably in the spring of 365 A.D.—though a later date, 367 A.D., is the one more usually assigned to the event—Valens issued an order for the expulsion of all the different bishops, who, after their banishment by Constantius, had been restored by Julian, implying thereby that he proposed to follow the Arian views of Constantius. In his advocacy of Arianism and persecution of the orthodox he was abetted by Albia Dominica, his wife. This order of expulsion would appear to have reached Alexandria on May 5th, and created a popular tumult, which was only appeased by the Prefect's promising on June 8th that the case of

Athanasius should be referred to the Emperor. On October 5th, however—no doubt from private information which he had received—Athanasius left his residence in the immediate neighbourhood of the church of St. Dionysius, and retired to a country-house near the New River.

This, says Theodoret, was the *fifth* time that Athanasius was driven from his Church.

CHAPTER XXII
His Fifth Brief Exile and Return

We learn from Socrates (iv. 13) that Athanasius concealed himself for four months in his father's tomb (cf. Soz., vi. 12). His retreat was only just in time; for the Prefect (who had probably played him false in the first instance) with an officer of the staff, and a company of soldiers, surrounded the church of St. Dionysius during that same night, broke open the doors, and searched the building in every direction, from the base to the roof, in the hope of discovering Athanasius. The search, of course, proved a fruitless one. The archbishop lay in concealment for four months, until, at the end of that time, an imperial notary, named Barasides or Bresidas, came—with an order for his return to his diocese—to the hiding-place where he lay concealed, attended by a large multitude, and led Athanasius back again to his Church, February 1st, 366 A.D.

And now ensued a period of comparative peace and quietness at Alexandria. The storm, however, continued to rage in the neighbouring Churches round about him. Eighty innocent presbyters, who had gone on an embassy to the Emperor when at Nicomedia to complain of their sufferings, were, by the Emperor's orders to the Prefect Modestus, put on board a vessel, which the crew, taking to their boats, set on fire, and all the eighty perished.

This tranquillity at Alexandria could hardly be said to have been broken by the pagan riot on July 21st of the same year, in which the Cæsarean Church, which George had completed before his death, was burned down; nor by the attempt of Lucius, on September 23, 367 A.D., to establish himself within the precincts of another church, in consequence of which the magistrates, in order to screen him from the effects of the popular fury, placed him in the hands of the military, that he might be conveyed away from Egypt.

Athanasius now enjoyed a certain amount of leisure and repose, which he could devote either to literary work, or to the regulation of the affairs of his diocese. His "Festal Letter" for 367 A.D.—"which (we are told) had been known from Greek MSS. long before the discovery of the series," and of which a Syriac translation has been also discovered—contains a list of the Books of the New Testament, which exactly agrees with our own, and also a list of the Books of the Old Testament. The Canonical Books are there spoken of as "The fountains of salvation, that he who thirsteth may be satisfied with the words they contain ('living words,' Syriac version). In these alone is proclaimed the doctrine of godliness. Let no man add to them, neither let him take aught from them." A second class of books is referred to as "read in Church for religious edification;" and the title "Apocryphal" is kept for a third class, to which heretical teachers have attributed an unreal importance. "assigning to them a date, and producing them as ancient writings, that thereby they might find occasion to lead astray the simple" (cf. Canon Westcott's "The Bible in the Church," 158, *seq.*).

To this period has been ascribed a treatise that is called "On the Incarnation and Against the Arians," which is a commentary on certain doctrinal passages, but which is not regarded by many as genuine. The doubts as to its genuineness have arisen from its speaking of "Three Hypostases," though in his next work he regards "Hypostasis" as identical with "essence;" and also from its referring St. John 14:28, not as he had done in "Orat.," i. 58, to the Divine Son-ship, but, like Dionysius, Cyril, and the Latins, to the assumed Humanity. "On the whole (it has been said) it seems most probable that this book was put together by an admirer and imitator of St. Athanasius—a disciple, so to speak, of his school, who might venture to differ from him on some points of exegesis or terminology, but would use, perhaps, to a considerable extent, memoranda of his teaching."

About the year 369 A.D. he convened a Council at Alexandria, in order that he might receive letters from a Roman Council held under Damasus, who was Liberius's successor, as well as from other bishops of the West, excommunicating Ursacius and Valens, and enforcing the authority of the Nicene Council.

Upon this Athanasius wrote a "Synodal Letter" addressed "to the Africans," that is, to those in the territory of Carthage, comparing the ten or twelve Synodical formularies or symbols of Arianism with the Creed of the Council of Nicæa, and exposing the attempt of its opponents to claim authority from the later proceedings of the Ariminian Council, as contra-distinguished from its earlier ones.

He wrote also another "Letter to Damasus," in

which he declares his astonishment that Auxentius, the Arian Bishop of Milan, had not been placed in the same category with Ursacius and Valens. This proposal was carried into effect by a Roman Synod afterwards held, and also by Synods in Gaul and Spain.

CHAPTER XXIII
The Closing Years of his Life

Athanasius about this time was called upon to excommunicate a violent and rapacious governor in Libya, and sent round a letter to say what he had done. One of these letters was addressed to Basil, who had very recently been appointed Archbishop of Cappadocian Cæsarea. He immediately informed his diocese of the sentence passed upon the governor, and wrote also a letter to Athanasius, in which he stated that the guilty person should not participate in any Church membership in his diocese, thus showing how strong was the bond of unity which existed between different Churches. This brought about a frequent interchange of letters between these two distinguished prelates in 371 A.D. And so it was that Basil consulted Athanasius respecting the unfortunate schism that prevailed at Antioch, and endeavoured to obtain advice and assistance from one whom he so highly valued for his earnest Christian sympathy, his deep discrimination, his practical ability, and his energy and promptness in action.

This correspondence between Athanasius and Basil is

of a deeply interesting nature—a correspondence carried on between the aged Athanasius and the youthful and active Basil, who was just entering on the direction of his new diocese. It is the sight (as Dean Stanley has well said, "E. C.," Lect. vii. 301) seldom witnessed, of a cordial salutation and farewell between the departing and the coming generation. The younger prelate, suspected of heresy, eagerly appeals to the old oracle of orthodoxy, and from him receives the welcome support which elsewhere he had sought in vain.

But though Athanasius was led to deal thus leniently with his friend Basil, and with his older friend Marcellus, yet he did not, in the closing days of his eventful life, relax at all in his strong opposition to anything which appeared to him erroneous in theory or doctrine concerning what may perhaps be spoken of as the human aspect of Christ's Incarnation.

Thus, in the different letters which he wrote about this time, we find him very careful to assert and maintain the true doctrine against all opponents.

(1.) We see him, in his "Letter to Adelphius," about 371 A.D., refuting the teaching of a certain set of Arians, and, in opposition to their views, supporting and defending the worship paid to the manhood of Christ, or, in other words, to His One Person Incarnate. Adelphius, to whom this letter was addressed, was Bishop of Onuphis, a town in the Delta. After returning from his exile in the Thebaid, he had taken his place in the Council of Alexandria.

In this letter Athanasius is very explicit as to the "Adoration due to Christ's Humanity as inseparable from His Divine Person:" and by its teaching, say the Benedictines, Athanasius plainly "condemns both Nestorius and Eutyches, long before the rise of their respective heresies. Nestorius, by saying that Christ is not to be divided into two; and Eutyches, by maintaining the nature of Christ to be entire and distinct." Towards the close of his short letter Athanasius writes:—"Therefore he who dishonours the temple, dishonours the Lord who dwells in the temple; and he who divides the Word from the body rejects the grace which was given to us in Him. And further, let not those most impious Ariomaniacs think that because the body is created, the Word also is a creature; nor let them, because the Word is not a creature, put a slur upon His body."

(2.) Again, in a "Letter to Maximus" in the same fear, he condemns those who spoke of the Man Christ Jesus as merely a Saint, with whom the Word was associated. Maximus, to whom this letter was addressed, was a Christian philosopher, a man of learning and piety, who had written to Athanasius respecting different heretical views concerning the Divinity of the Son. Some of the advocates of these false opinions had regarded the Incarnation as a mere association between the Word and Jesus Christ, while others had cast aside all the supernatural character of the Nativity.

Athanasius thus concludes his brief letter:—"Let the Confession of Faith, made by the Fathers at Nicæa, stand good; for it is correct, and capable of overthrowing any impious heresy, and especially the Arian, which insults the Word of God, and necessarily falls into impiety against the Holy Ghost."

(3.) And, once more, in his "Letter to Epictetus." the Bishop of Corinth—a letter which he wrote in reply to a communication from him—he protested most strongly against those who, while they professed their belief in the Confession of Nicæa, regarded the body of Christ as not truly human, but "formed out of the essence of the Godhead."

This—it has been remarked—was the second proposition of the Apollinarian heresy.

This letter is of very great interest as a specimen of Athanasius's farsighted theological capacity. It is a letter which theological writers and councils have alike quoted as an admirable exposition of the true doctrine on this question (see "Introd. Library of Fathers").

Athanasius thus concludes his letter:—"Thanks to the Lord, in proportion to the pain which we felt in reading your minutes, was our pleasure when we came to the end. For the parties separated in agreement with each other, and were at peace in the confession of the pious and orthodox faith. And this fact has persuaded me, after I had previously considered the matter at length, to write this short letter; for I took account of this, that possibly my silence might cause pain instead of joy to those who by their agreement gave us occasion for rejoicing."

It cannot but be felt and acknowledged that these and cognate theories—as was so often the case with heretical teaching—sprung from the desire to exalt, at any cost, the dignity of Christ. The advocates, however, of the Council of Nicæa clearly saw that such views were destructive of true opinions respecting the manhood of Christ, and that they were, in fact, a revival of the theories formerly held by the Docetæ, and that practically in their results they infringed on the true conception of Christ's Deity.

(4.) In the following year, 372 A.D., Athanasius attacked these views in two books, whose title is "Against Apollinaris." They are remarkable alike for their fulness of thought and matter, and for their keen and vigorous reasoning. But we do not find him mentioning the name of his old friend, the Bishop of Laodicea in Syria, as though he were responsible for these errors. Nor, indeed, in his letter to Epictetus had he made mention of his name; nor in two letters to friends written about the same time on the same subject. His strong desire to think the best he could of those who had been associated with him by the ties of friendship or of Common work, induced him to cast aside suspicions, which afterwards, perhaps, proved to be unhappily just. These different treatises seem, as it were, to have been forced from Athanasius, as though he felt that his brethren needed his opinions as a guide to them in their judgment on these novel statements of doctrine, and as though he feared that he himself might be induced to look leniently on erroneous views, at the dictate of private friendship. It would seem that Athanasius died in the conviction of his friend's orthodoxy, an opinion which a letter of Apollinaris seems certainly to favour, in which he speaks of the agreement in doctrine, as well as the friendly intercourse which existed between them to the last. It was not till several years after the death of Athanasius that the views of Apollinaris were condemned at Rome.

In these two books Christ is set forth in the clearest and most vigorous manner as "perfect God and perfect Man." It has been thought by some (as *e.g.* Macarius) that expressions of his in ii. 10 seem to be favourable to "Monothelitism;" but we find, from the surrounding context and the line of argument, that they were intended to signify that "the Divine Will in Christ was dominant over the human." If we find the expression that "God suffered through the flesh," it is subsequently explained by the general tone of the reasoning, in which he strongly opposed the idea of the Godhead of the Saviour being capable of suffering. We may, indeed, object to certain statements not being worded with sufficient accuracy and care, but the whole argument shows us that his teaching is sound and correct. These treatises of his, which he published towards the close of his life, clearly prove that he rejected by anticipation—as we have before remarked in regard to other views—those heresies in reference to the Nature and the Person of Christ, which disturbed the Christian Church during the next three centuries.

The books against Apollinaris may be shown by internal evidence to have a striking affinity to the three letters which have just been brought under our notice.

It has been forcibly said, that "Apollinarianism is one of the most melancholy phenomena of Church history, as a heretical reaction against heresy, conducted by a bishop of rare ability, respected and even loved by typical Churchmen for his services to historic Christianity, and animated, even in the speculations which misled him, by a religious zeal for the majesty of Christ; a reaction also which not only did fatal mischief by destroying faith in the Redeemer's real Humanity, but also provoked an equally calamitous revulsion in the direction of a denial of His Personal Oneness."

Athanasius was "in truth the *Immortal*" ("Christ. Rememb.," xxxvii. 206), in respect of the fruits and results of his labours. He was, as it were, continually "planting trees under which men of a later age might sit."

The years of his life were now fast drawing to a close. He was, nevertheless, still in harness, still vigorous. They were years which had been zealously, earnestly, and unremittingly employed in the service of his Master, ever since those youthful days in which he had been received into the house of his first friend and patron, Bishop Alexander.

After a life of contest (so writes the distinguished author of "The Arians," ch. vi.) prolonged, in spite of the hardships he encountered, beyond the age of seventy years, he fell asleep in peaceable possession of the Churches for which he suffered. It so happened, through the good providence of God, that the fury of persecution, heavily as it threatened in his last years, was suspended till his death, when it at once burst forth upon the Church with renewed vigour. Thus he was permitted to muse over his past services and his prospects of the future; to collect his mind to meet his God, gathering himself up with Jacob on his bed of age, and peacefully yielding up the ghost. Yet, amid the decay of nature, and the visions of coming dissolution, the attention of Athanasius was in no wise turned from the duties of his station. His resolute resistance of heresy had been but one portion of his services; a more excellent praise is due to him for his charitable skill in binding together his brethren in unity. The Church of Alexandria was the natural mediator between the East and the West; and Athanasius had well improved the advantage committed to him.

He died in the spring of the year 373 A.D.—a date which appears certain, as supported by the "Festal Index," the Maffeian Fragment, and by other ancient and modern authorities. It was, perhaps, on Thursday, May the 2nd (according to the calendar of the Greek and Latin Churches), that he was taken to his rest. His successor, Cyril, tells us that he had occupied the episcopal chair at Alexandria for forty-six years. Had he lived a few weeks longer his episcopate would have lasted forty-seven years. After having recommended one of his presbyters, named Peter, as his successor, he quietly passed away under the shelter of his own roof. He had been called upon to undergo "many struggles" (Rufin., ii. 3). His earthly lot had been full of vexation and unrest; and his life, in the words of Tillemont, had been a "continual martyrdom." He was buried in Alexandria, though his body was afterwards transferred to Constantinople. "The story"—says Professor Bright, to whose researches no biographer of Athanasius can fail to owe the deepest obligations—"the story of its removal by a Venetian captain in 1454 to Santa Croce in Venice, reads like a strange echo of some of his adventures during life."

Gregory Nazianzen thus refers to his death:—

"He ended his life in a holy old age, and went to keep company with his fathers, the patriarchs, prophets, apostles, and martyrs, who had fought valiantly for the truth, as he had done.

CHAPTER XXIV
His Character as a Man

(1.) In estimating the character of Athanasius we cannot but notice in the first place the deep tone of piety and holiness which marked all his thoughts, words, and works. This characteristic is conspicuous alike in all his writings and in all his controversies, as well as in all the actions of his life. They were all conducted as a sincere Christian would be likely to conduct them. He felt deeply and overpoweringly that he was Christ's servant; and all that he did bore the impress of his sincere convictions on this point.[14]

(2.) His natural temperament—like that of Chrysostom—was no doubt sensitive to a high degree; but, nevertheless, his character was conspicuous for its resolution and fixedness of aim and object. He determinedly carried out the end which he had deliberately placed before him, however much he might have been affected by his sympathies for others, and by the impression which other natures made upon him. And so, though never swerving from the great principles

---

[14] "Athanase etait enflammé, dès sa jeunesse, de la passion qui fait les Saints, l'amour de Jésus Christ."—De Broglie.

which guided him, and the great objects which he had placed before him, he was enabled to "combine firmness with discretion and discrimination," and to be, in a good and Scriptural sense, "all things to all men."

(3.) And again, we can trace in him that deep tenderness of disposition which rendered him so faithful and loving a friend, so ready to cast the ægis of his protection over others, so desirous to secure peace and unity—a trait in his character which, in response, caused him to be loved with so true a loyalty and such unalterable affection by those placed under him, namely, his hundred suffragans, his clergy, the monks, and the laity.

(4.) But there is another aspect in which we ought to regard the life of Athanasius. We may cease for a while to look upon him, subjectively, as the Saint, and consider him as the great and undaunted antagonist, not only of an Arianizing Church, but also of most of the emperors who occupied for the time being the throne of the Cæsars. It is this aspect of his character which invests him with so deep an interest, and brings so prominently into the foreground all that is grand and heroic in his nature. So remarkable was this characteristic of Athanasius, that he may fairly be said to be the one only Christian saint who has inflamed with a glow of enthusiastic admiration the cold, cynical nature of the critical author of the "Decline and Fall." Though he was supported by his own party, yet it has been truly said by Dean Stanley, "that he was one of those strong characters who render to others a stronger support than others can ever render to them."

At the Council of Nicæa he had stood almost alone in opposition to the Meletian sectaries, and, though he bravely battled for what he deemed to be right, it was probably well for the peace of the Church that he did not prevail.

Again, in all the later struggles in which he was engaged, he stood almost alone and isolated in his conflict with the Arian party, and scarcely obtained any support from those who occupied the highest places either in Church or State. The Arians had gained the ear of emperors; had acquired a potent voice in all the councils of the Church; and numbered in their ranks many of those who were the most distinguished men of the day, either by reason of the offices which they held, or from the talents and learning they possessed. He here stood out with all boldness against any concession to the great or the powerful when the cause of truth was at stake. In such a case he was "Athanasius contra mundum." He came forward as courageously and undauntedly in his vindication of the truth as Elijah had done of old on Mount Carmel in the conflict for the truth which he waged with a ruthless king and a dominant hierarchy. It is this aspect of his character which Hooker has brought out so forcibly in his magnificent eulogy upon him:—"Only of Athanasius there was nothing observed through that long tragedy, other than such as very well became a wise man to do, and a righteous to suffer. So that this was the plain condition of those times; the whole world against Athanasius, and Athanasius against it. Half a hundred years spent in doubtful trial, which of the two in the end would prevail; the side which had all, or else the part which had no friend but God and death." The proverb, "Athanasius contra mundum" is one, "which, though few are worthy to claim it for themselves, yet all may well take to heart as a warning against confounding popularity with truth, or isolation with heresy, or temporary depression with lasting defeat." The struggle which Athanasius carried on with Constantine, Constantius, Julian, and Valens has been well, but briefly, recorded by Gibbon; and it has been worked out at greater length in the pages of Tillemont. The details of this struggle are, it must be confessed, often involved and intricate, and not unfrequently somewhat wearisome; but, in its general spirit and features, the contest contains many valuable and instructive lessons. We cannot fail to see in this long conflict which he waged with the imperial power, and which the imperial power waged with him, strong evidence that there was a degree of freedom in the Christian Church which had ceased to exist in other functions and offices of the State. Such an individual manifestation of independence had scarcely ever been exhibited before. Until the time of Athanasius, subservience, or, perhaps, servility, was the favourite quality of courtiers and those in high position. Thus he won from Julian the designation of the "meddling demagogue," the "audacious conspirator;" showing clearly the Emperor's personal antipathy to him, in consequence of his independence of character.

We may remark also, that the charges generally preferred against him were of a personal nature. It was not for heresy or false doctrine that he was brought before the Council of Tyre, but on purely personal charges; such, *e.g.*, as the alleged murder of Arsenius; the breaking of a sacred chalice; conspiracy against the Emperor; the consecration of a church without the Emperor's sanction; the detention of corn at Alexandria; the fact of procuring his restoration to his diocese by the order of the Emperor, after having been deposed by a Council; his alleged correspondence with Magnentius— charges of a personal character which he was able thoroughly to confute and repudiate. But though the charges brought against him were thus of a personal character, yet they had their origin in the theological rancour and malevolence of the Arian party against him. "Athanasius"—so writes Dean Milman ("H. of C.," iii. v.)—"stands out as the prominent character of the period, in the history, not merely of Christianity, but of the world. That history is one long controversy; the life of Athanasius one unwearied and incessant strife. It is neither the serene course of a being elevated by his religion above the cares and tumults of ordinary life, nor the restless activity of one perpetually employed in a conflict with the ignorance, vice, and misery of an unconverted people. Yet even now the memory of Athanasius is regarded by many wise and good men with reverence, which, in Catholic countries, is actual adoration; in Protestant, approaches towards it."

(5.) The qualities, however, which would appear to have arrested the attention of the men of his day in the greatest degree were the *versatility* of his character, and the *ready promptitude* with which he was able to act in emergencies.

He would seem to have possessed those marvellous natural powers which enabled him—as Themistocles is pictured by Thucydides (i. 138)—to determine at a moment's notice what was best to be done. It was this remarkable versatility which rendered his character so many-sided. The same great historian (ii. 41) assigns this peculiar grace of character to the Athenians—the power of adapting themselves with the happiest versatility to all the different circumstances in which they might be placed. It was thus that he, like the great Apostle, could "make himself all things to all men," without losing the uprightness and firmness of his character. In this respect

St. Augustine resembled him. This peculiar aspect of his character struck very forcibly Gregory Nazianzen, and he has brought it out very pointedly in his Eulogy— saying of him that he could equally distribute praise or blame; that he could arouse the sluggish, and repress the enthusiastic; that, while single in his aims, he was manifold in his modes of government; that he was wise in his speech, and yet still wiser in his thoughts and intentions; that he was on a level with the most ordinary men, and could rise to the height of the most speculative; and that he united in himself all the various attributes of all the heathen gods.

(6.) He was, moreover, master of a caustic humour, which is frequently observable in his life. We have already described his ready retort to Constantius, when, prompted by the Arians, the Emperor asked him to grant their party a church for their own worship at Alexandria:—"I will grant (he said) a church to the heretics at Alexandria, if you will grant one to the orthodox at Antioch." Again, we have seen the pointed and sarcastic humour with which he produced the muffled figure of Arsenius—whose amputated hand had been exposed to view in a box by the Arians—at the Council of Tyre, and said to the assembly, after drawing out from under the cloak first one hand and then the other—"I presume that no one thinks that God has given to any man more than two hands!" Again, when he was once asked his judgment respecting death-bed baptism, he did not argue the matter, but replied in an apologue which was irresistible:—"An angel once said to my great predecessor, Peter, why do you send me these sacks (wind-bags) carefully sealed up, with nothing whatever inside?" And, once more, we see the same spirit of raillery in his answers to those who upbraided him with cowardice in avoiding the violence of his enemies by flight:—"Thus they reproach me with my present flight, not for the sake of my character, as wishing me to show my manliness by coming forward (how is it possible that such a wish can be entertained by enemies in behalf of those who run not with them in the same career of madness?); but being full of malice, they pretend this, and whisper up and down that such is the case, thinking, foolish as indeed they are, that through fear of their revilings, I shall yet be induced to give myself up to them. For this is what they desire: to accomplish this they have recourse to all kinds of schemes: they pretend themselves to be friends, while they search after me as enemies, to the end that they may glut themselves with my blood, and put me also out of the way, because I have always opposed, and do still oppose, their impiety, and confute and brand their heresy" ("Apol. pro Fugâ," § 2).

(7.) There was another feature in his character, which his opponents assigned to the magical power they were fond of attributing to him. It was this: the rapid and mysterious nature of his movements from place to place; his power (like that of Themistocles) of rapidly divining beforehand what was going to take place; and the humour with which he sometimes played upon the credulity and the fears of men. We can trace this rapidity of movement and sudden Elijah-like presentation of himself when least expected, in the manner in which he placed himself suddenly in the way before the Emperor at Constantinople, refusing to let him pass till he had promised to grant him his petition. It was thus he could foretell what was likely to come to pass. When his brethren at Alexandria were hopeless at the accession of Julian to the throne, he merely remarked—"It is but a little cloud, which will soon pass away." We have seen him being pursued by his enemies in a boat up the Nile. They see another boat coming down the stream, and ask, "Where is Athanasius?" The answer is returned, "He is not very far off"—probably by Athanasius himself, certainly by one of the crew of the boat in which he was at the time. Again, while he is passing through one of the squares in Alexandria, and while the crowd is standing round, a crow is seen to fly above their heads. They jestingly ask him to divine what its croak presignified. "Do you not hear?" he replied. "It is saying 'Cras,' 'Cras,' the Latin for 'to-morrow,' and it implies that *to-morrow* something unsatisfactory will happen, for your heathen festival will be put down to-morrow by an imperial edict." The event predicted came to pass; and no doubt the crowd ascribed his foreknowledge to magical powers (Soz., iv. 10). We, indeed, can trace this power of Athanasius to the true causes from which it sprung, namely, to his marvellous rapidity of movement from place to place; to his varied sources of information amongst all ranks of men; and to his notorious quickness of observation and perception. But we can easily understand that, in that age—and not in that age only—all this might naturally have been assigned to the power of magic and witchcraft, which they believed him to possess, and which many would not cease to believe was the actuating cause of all that took place in the case of Arsenius, since there were many "who maintained that it was an optical delusion, caused by the glamour which Athanasius had cast over the Council. And thus even an intellectual heathen— Ammianus Marcellinus (xv. 7)—was convinced that Athanasius's knowledge of the future was derived from arts of divination and from the auguries of birds" (cf.

Stanley, "E. C.," vii. 288).

(8.) It was not merely, says Bishop Wordsworth ("C. H." ii. 29), the learning, courage, and matchless fortitude of Athanasius that make his life and ministry a worthy subject for careful meditation and devout study; but it was also his wisdom and patience, and his kindness and charity, that entitle him to admiration. Thus Gregory Nazianzen ("Orat.," xxi. 31) remarks, that Athanasius blended the properties of two precious stones, and was a diamond to those who struck him, and a magnet to those who differed from him, thus combining "magnetic attractiveness with adamantine firmness"; and dwells on his conciliatory spirit and love of peace. This, he maintains, is preferable to many vigils, and to nights spent in lying on the gravel, which things terminate with those who use them; adding that this conciliatory spirit was not of less value than all his banishments.

(9.) In his heroism there was not a spark of fanaticism. He knew full well when to resist and when to yield. He was "noble not only in fight, but in flight." When Constantius sought to apprehend him, he felt how needful to the Church his own life was, and while he retired from danger, he entrusted the care of his flock temporarily to others, in the hope and expectation of returning to them-once more in better times.

(10.) His forbearance and gentleness were most conspicuous. When those around him indulged in passionate invectives against those who had fallen from the orthodox faith, he was ever ready to make excuses for their defection. When Hilary (cf. "Fragments," vi. 678) poured the vials of his indignation upon Liberius of Rome for his fall into error, and uttered anathemas upon him, we find Athanasius writing of him ("Ad Monach.,"

§ 41) in a spirit of love, and pity, and regret, and thus heaping coals of fire on his head. When Hosius fell away under the fire of persecution, he gently expressed his commiseration for one bowed down by age and suffering. Again, we can trace the gentleness of Athanasius by contrasting his conduct with that of Lucifer of Cagliari, in the case of those who had lapsed at Ariminum. While the former, as we have seen, was ready at the Council at Alexandria to readmit into communion those who had fallen away from the truth under the pressure of persecution, if they were willing to renounce their error and express their penitence for their past conduct, the latter not only refused to receive them back again into Church communion, but branded their ministrations with infamy. It has been truly said by Canon Robertson ("Ch. Hist.," ii. i. 295), that "his unbending steadiness of purpose was united with a rare skill in dealing with men; he knew when to give way as well as when to make a show of resistance."

(11.) Moreover we should be led to form an imperfect idea of the lofty, noble, courageous, and yet affectionate and gentle character of Athanasius, if we did not take into consideration the state of the age in which he lived, and the condition of the people with whom he was thrown into contact. The character of the Greeks had greatly degenerated from the standard to which it had once attained. It had grown fickle, faithless, debased, with no sincerity, no earnestness of purpose. The great Roman satirist had already described in scathing language their vices and their follies; nor, indeed, had he dwelt in less caustic terms on Egyptian fanaticism, profligacy, and violence. By contrast, therefore, with his environment, the character of Athanasius stands forth all the more grandly; the dark background in which it is set tending to display, in brighter and fairer light, its beauty and attractiveness.

(12.) Athanasius was not, of course, without blemish and without fault. He was but a man after all, though a very exalted specimen of a man. He might sometimes be led away into acrimonious severity in controversy; he might not always interpret aright, or even, perhaps, charitably, the motives and principles of those who were opposed to him on the great fundamental doctrines to which he attached so deep an importance; he may, perhaps, have sometimes fallen into a casuistical line of argument; he may have been chargeable, now and then, with errors in judgment, or possibly in conduct; but still we cannot refrain from placing him among the very foremost and noblest characters that have adorned the religion of Christ since the days in which the Apostles lived and taught.

"The narrative of his life," as it has been truly remarked by Möhler, "is a panegyric which words can only enfeeble."

CHAPTER XXV
His Character as a Theologian

From the consideration of the more active and practical side of the life of Athanasius we would pass to the more intellectual aspect of his character. He may fairly be regarded, not only as the most eminent theologian of his age, but, in a certain sense, of all ages. The distinguished reputation of Hosius of Cordova passed away, to a great extent, with his life; but not so that of Athanasius, which grew and developed as time flowed on, and had attained to such ample proportions in the next generation, that he then claimed from the world the epithet of "Great." Nor was his eminent reputation confined to the East, it spread also to the West. In this respect none of the Eastern Fathers could be compared to him. He had lived for a long period during exile both at Rome and in Treves. He had acquired a knowledge of the Latin language, in order that he might enjoy more familiar intercourse with the Bishop of Rome and other friends there.

The strictly logical and argumentative style of his writing was even more adapted to the calm, dispassionate, and thoughtful Romans, than the more rhetorical and imaginative compositions of the Eastern Church usually were. It is probably the deep impression which his style of composition and tone of mind made upon the Western Church, that caused the "Athanasian Creed" to be generally ascribed to him, not only throughout the middle ages, but even by our own Reformers. It is now commonly supposed to be either of French or Spanish origin. It could not certainly be fairly attributed to Athanasius, since there are different words and expressions to be found in it which were unknown to him, and since it clearly asserts the doctrine of the double procession of the Spirit—a doctrinal statement, which, it is said, does not occur in his writings, and to which, possibly, he might not have given his sanction.

Athanasius has been well described as the "Father of all Theology," and as the "Founder of Orthodoxy."

It may fairly be asserted, that before the settlement of the Creed of Nicæa, in which he was the principal actor, the specific idea of orthodox doctrine was unknown. Theological views were not only too simple, but too unformed and transitional to allow of its existence. He, on the contrary, introduced an elaborate and minute statement of doctrinal truth, which was of so precise and definite a character, that it may have led to the idea that he was originally a lawyer.

But though his intense love of doctrinal truth, and his earnest desire to maintain the orthodox view in opposition to the errors of Arianism, may have hurried him occasionally into a violence of language which we should scarcely have expected to find in his writings, and should not associate with his evenly-balanced and argumentative cast of mind, yet they never led him into cruel or merciless action, such as that into which his successor, Cyril, was hurried. Athanasius could never have been charged with any participation whatever in the murder of Bishop George; but Cyril is by no means acquitted of complicity with the cruel and savage butchery of Hypatia. Athanasius was never guilty of persecution. It was his ruling idea, that "the duty of orthodoxy is not to compel, but to persuade belief." Cyril, however, placed himself at the head of ferocious monks and violent partisans, and carried out his schemes by force and coercion.

The centre of his theological scheme was the doctrine of the *Incarnation*. This was the subject of his earliest treatise, which gives us his calm and practical estimate of the doctrine, before he was actually engaged in the Arian controversy. On this point his teaching reached far beyond the limits of his own day. He speaks of the Incarnation of the Son of God as essential to the recovery of fallen man, and also of the fitness and propriety of man's being taught by Him, who is the wisdom of the Father. His language in reference to Redemption is in perfect conformity with Scripture.

Another feature in the theological character of Athanasius is to be traced in the masterly manner in which he could discriminate between mere imaginary differences, and in which he could draw a line of separation between what is essential and what is non-essential. Such discrimination he exhibited in allaying the disputes and differences which arose between the monks and the hermits, which seemed at one time likely to imperil the stability of the Eastern Church, just as the feuds between the Franciscans and Dominicans in the Western Church provoked the most serious disturbances. He lived among both: at one time in the cell of the contemplative anchorite, at another amidst the social life of some cœnobitic fraternity. Here, remarks Gregory Nazianzen, he showed himself the great reconciler of the age, "imitating Him who by His own blood set at peace those who had parted asunder; showing (with the hermits) that religion was able to become philosophical, and (with the monks) that philosophy stood in need of the guidance of religion." And not in discipline only, but also in doctrine, he proved very clearly that he was willing to sacrifice the letter to the spirit ("Orat.," xxi. 19). By a decree of the Nicene Council, it was ordered that not less than three bishops should be present at the ordination of a bishop, while another decree prescribed that such an appointment should be sanctioned at Alexandria. We find, however, that when a young and active layman of the name of Siderius had been consecrated by a single bishop, and without any consultation with the Bishop of Alexandria, Athanasius not only acquiesced in the appointment—though in contravention of the rules handed down by antiquity—but yielded also to the exigencies of the times, and promoted him to the principal see of the province.

Again, in regard to the term "Homöousion," we can scarcely believe that he could have valued any other theological expression more highly—an expression which he had himself been very instrumental in introducing into the Creed of the Nicene Council; nor did he ever swerve from the truths that underlie that term. And yet, at one time, he was even willing for a season to forego its use, when he found that it was misunderstood and misconceived.

Thus, again, at the Council of Alexandria, in 362 A.D., we find him endeavouring to reconcile divisions between the Eastern and Western Churches, and to establish—as was done at the Council of the Apostles at

Jerusalem—"not an enforcement of uniformity, but a toleration of diversity." His object, at that period, was to unite the Church together, which had been rent asunder in the protracted contest with Arianism. It was consequently determined by this Council, over which Athanasius presided, that those who had lapsed into Arianism should, on their submission, be received back again into the Church. To this proposal the "fierce Sardinian," Lucifer of Cagliari, was the sole opponent.

One other subject was treated of in this same Council at Alexandria. The dispute which had commenced at the Council of Nicæa, respecting the signification of the word "Hypostasis," culminated at the time of the Council of Alexandria. The Western Church continued to use the word in the same sense as that in which it was employed at the Nicene Council, viz., as equivalent to "Ousia," and translated it by the term "Substantia;" but the Eastern Church had now began to use it in a different sense, namely that of "Prosôpon," or "Person," and attacked the Latins with the charge of Sabellianism for their use of it, while the Latins made a counter-charge of Arianism against the Greeks for the meaning in which they employed the term. We learn from Socrates (iii. 7), that in order to put an end to this controversy, it was suggested that these terms should be altogether abandoned. It was then that Athanasius exhibited the judgment and discernment for which, as a theologian, he was so remarkable. We hear from Gregory Nazianzen ("Orat.," xxi.) that "The controversy had reached such a pitch, that the two quarters of the world were on the point of being torn asunder by a difference of syllables. When Athanasius, of blessed memory, saw and heard this, he, like a true man of God—like a grand steward of souls—determined that this absurd and irrational division of the Divine Word was not to be endured; and the remedy, the charm which he had in his own character and mind, he brought to bear on the disease. How did he effect this? He called both sides together. He addressed them gently and kindly. He explained in exact terms the sense of what was intended; and when he found that they agreed, and had no difference in what they meant, he granted freely to each the use of their words and names; whilst he bound them together by the things and facts which the words represented. This was more profitable than all the long labours and discourses, in which, perhaps, there may have been an element of ambition and vanity. This is more honourable than all the sleepless nights and hard couches, of which the advantage ends with the endurance. This was worth all his famous wanderings and exiles; for this was the object for which he bore those sufferings, and to which he devoted himself after those sufferings were over."

The Council of Alexandria was the last occasion of a public character on which Athanasius came before the world. It is a pleasing thought—as Dean Stanley ("E. C." Lect. vii.) has remarked—that the last public acts of Athanasius's life were of wisdom, discernment, and charity.

The intricate question of the "Hypostasis" has received a careful investigation at the hands of the learned and subtle author of "The Arians," (ch. v. § 2). He has remarked that the word "Person," which we venture to use in speaking of those three distinct manifestations of Himself, which it has pleased Almighty God to give us, is, in its philosophical sense, too wide for our meaning. Its essential signification, as applied to ourselves, is that of an individual intelligent agent, answering to the Greek "Hypostasis," or "reality." On the other hand, if we restrict it to its etymological sense of "persona" or "prosôpon," *i.e.*, "character," it evidently means less than the Scripture doctrine which we wish to ascertain by it; denoting merely certain outward expressions of the Supreme Being relatively to ourselves, which are of an accidental and variable nature. The statements of Revelation then lie between this internal and external view of the Divine Essence, between Tritheism, and what is popularly called Unitarianism.

In the choice of difficulties then, between words which say too much and too little, the *Latins*, looking at the popular and practical side of the doctrine, selected a term expressive of the external and defective notion of the Son and Spirit, and called them 'Personæ," or (literally) "Characters;" with no intention, however, of infringing on the doctrine of their completeness and reality, as distinct from the Father, but aiming at the whole truth, as nearly as their language would permit. The *Greeks*, on the other hand, with their instinctive anxiety for philosophical accuracy of expression, secured the notion of their existence in themselves, by calling them "Hypostases" or "Realities;" for which they considered with some reason, that they had the sanction of the writer of the Epistle to the Hebrews (1:3). Moreover, they were led to insist upon this internal view of the doctrine, by the prevalence of Sabellianism in the East in the third century; a heresy, which professed to resolve the distinction of the Three Persons, into a mere distinction of character. Hence the prominence given to the "Three Hypostases" (the "Three Realities") in the Creeds of the Semi-Arians (*e.g.* Lucian's and Basil's, A.D. 341–358) who were the special antagonists of

Sabellius, Marcellus, Photinus, and kindred heretics. It was this praiseworthy jealousy of the Sabellians, which obliged the Greeks to lay stress upon the doctrine of the Word in real existence, lest the bare use of the terms, Word, Voice, Power, Wisdom, and Radiance in designating our Lord, should lead to a forgetfulness of His personality. At the same time, the word "Ousia" ("substance") was adopted by them, to express the simple individuality of the Divine nature, to which the Greeks, as scrupulously as the Latins, referred the separate personalities of the Son and Spirit. Thus the two great divisions of Christendom rested satisfied each with its own theology, agreeing in doctrine, though differing in the expression of it.

Athanasius, without caring to be uniform in his use of terms about which the orthodox differed, favours the Latin usage, speaking of the Supreme Being as one "Hypostasis," *i.e.*, "substance." Such was the state of the controversy at the time of the Alexandrian Council; the Church of Antioch being, as it were, the stage upon which the two parties in dispute were represented, the Meletians siding with the orthodox of the East, and the Eustathians with those of the West. The Council, however, instead of taking part with either, determined, in accordance with the writings of Athanasius himself, that, since the question merely related to the usage of words, it was expedient to allow Christians to understand the "Hypostasis" in one or other sense indifferently.

In vindicating and defending the doctrine of the Holy Trinity, Athanasius is most careful to guard it from all error and misconception in every point of view. But he regarded it as a great mystery. He did not, therefore, attempt to explain away the deep mysteriousness that naturally enveloped the doctrine. Nor did he aim at defining or elucidating it beyond the limit to which Holy Scriptures goes on this point. He felt in his own mind that its opponents could start captious and casuistical objections against the doctrine in some of its aspects. He refuted all the different objections which admitted of such a refutation; but all the specious, vain, and cunningly-devised arguments, which the over-refinement and casuistry of the Oriental mind, trained in the schools of Alexandria, and conversant with Greek philosophy, advanced against the doctrine, he did not care to answer, nor did he attempt to refute. His final appeal was to the Word of God.

It is very natural that in the case of a man so absorbed as Athanasius was during his whole life with one single controversy, the works that he wrote and left behind him of a really valuable and instructive character should, for the most part, be those which treat of this particular subject, which occupied for so long a time all his thoughts and influenced all his actions. We can hardly suppose that he could have concentrated his thoughts in an equal degree on other topics, and argued with similar force on them. Nor, again, can we wonder, if this particular controversy gave a bias and a direction to all his views. Thus, for example, when he describes Arianism as the unpardonable sin, we can now clearly see that he was unintentionally wresting Scripture to suit the particular doctrine and line of thought which filled all the field of his vision. But it was an infirmity in a great and good man which we should be disposed to treat with leniency, and to pardon as the natural outcome of all that he saw and felt. He could trace in Arianism everything that was cruel, crafty, tyrannical, ambitious, and mean. He firmly believed it to be a

heresy that insulted the majesty of God, and derogated
from the divinity of Christ; and seeing this, we can
scarcely be surprised to find him regarding it as the
unpardonable sin. It was a mistake, no doubt, but it was
a natural one; nor jean we be greatly astonished that his
mind, with all its strength, simplicity, and truthfulness,
should have fallen into such an error in Scriptural
exegesis. The very warmth of his affections, the depth of
his piety, his ardent love for God and Christ, might all
tend to foster such a conviction in his mind.

Athanasius, as we have already remarked, had been a
diligent reader of Plato and of Homer; and the energy
and incisiveness of his style would lead to the inference
that he had also studied Demosthenes. But he had no
ambition to excel in merely showy and epideictic
oratory. He was master of a calm and irresistible logic.
The rhetorical displays of the Sophists had no charm for
him. He was not led away from the subject before him
into the utterance of angry and revengeful philippics in
the pulpit against his opponents. Bitterly tried and
tempted as he might have been by the cruel treatment
which he received, yet he never indulged in any mere
manifestation of ill-will against calumniators or
enemies.

If we seek to trace to its source the great moral power
and influence of Athanasius, we shall find it in the depth
of his communion with God; a communion realised in
the Scriptures. He was an earnest, prayerful student of
the Word of God. It was the remark of Gregory
Nazianzen, that he was better acquainted with both the
Old and New Testaments than others were with one. He
devoted himself to the daily study of the Sacred
Scriptures, and especially of the Psalms, on which he
published commentaries and practical expositions.

Hence the strength of his devout and earnest piety. In a letter which he wrote to his friend Marcellinus, he says, "I learn that you give yourself up to the study of all the Sacred Scriptures, and particularly of the Psalms;" adding, "I praise you greatly for this; my own desire is earnestly directed to that especial portion of Holy Scripture, and indeed to all the sacred writings."

That he held this constant communion with God, both in prayer and in meditation, and in the Holy Sacrament, we learn from the history of his life. How often do we see him, in the midst of peril and persecution, betaking himself to the seclusion of the desert, or finding repose in the peaceful services of the monks. His modesty and meekness were singularly conspicuous. He ever deemed others better than himself. An admirer has said of him, that "he united childlike simplicity and playful cheerfulness, with philosophic wisdom, theological science, political sagacity, saintly piety, and heroic magnanimity." And another has remarked, "His zeal for the consubstantiality had its root in his loyalty to the consubstantial."

"The vital centre of Christianity (says Dorner) is grasped by Athanasius with such intense fervour, and is treated in such a scientific spirit, that it gives us the ground-work of a grand system of speculative theology." And again, "Athanasius the Great made it the work of his long and eventful life to defend the Creed put forth by the Nicene Council, with all the weapons of science and spiritual chivalry, against the vacillating and short-sighted on the one side, and the apostate on the other; and to him was given the happiness of seeing that to which he had devoted his life attain ever-widening influence and recognition, and to sink into his grave crowned with honour, and laden with the fruit of his labours."

APPENDIX
On Arianism and Semi-Arianism

(1.) Arianism, as represented by Eudoxius, or Aetius, or Eunomius, denied not only the "Homöousion," but also the "Homöiousion." Thus its advocates were styled "Anomœans," or sometimes "Heterousians," inasmuch as in their estimation the Son was *unlike* the Father, and in substance and essence differed from him.

But, as was naturally to be expected, many members of the Arian party were unwilling to go to so great a length as this, and desired to find some intermediate standpoint between the extremes of Arianism and the doctrine of Athanasius, on which they might take up their position.

Hence arose semi-Arianism, advocated by Basil of Ancyra. At a Council held there in 358 A.D., a profession of faith was published, which erred on the side of defect rather than on that of excess. It would appear that both Athanasius and Hilary were disposed to regard this exposition of the faith with a certain degree of indulgence. It did not, indeed, include all that they might have desired. It might not be perfect in its development of doctrine. But still, so far as it went, it claimed their sympathy; and those who held it might fairly be regarded as not being very far from the truth; and for a short period semi-Arianism was in the ascendant. The advocates of exteme Arianism were banished, and Constantius entertained the scheme of summoning a Council at Nicomedia, at which the doctrine of semi-Arianism might be officially proclaimed as the doctrine of the Church. But, nevertheless, the victory of semi-Arianism was not long-lived. It soon became apparent that there was no trustworthy ground of belief between the extreme of Arianism on the one hand, and of the Athanasian Creed on the other.

The result of the successes which the semi-Arians had gained was the natural one that often befalls a victorious party. Divisions followed in the wake of success. The party, apparently united before, was now split into different factions. And such diversities in faith and doctrine gradually paved the way for Macedonianism, which denied the divine consubstantiality of the Holy Ghost, and for Apollinarianism, which imagined that, in the Person of Christ, the divine mind was to be substituted for the reasonable soul.

Though at first the Council at Ariminum (Rimini), A.D. 359, seemed to be favourable to the Athanasian party, yet by chicanery and fraud[15] its decisions proved in the end to correspond with the formula drawn up at Sirmium—a Creed inspired by the Emperor. Thus, said Jerome, "The world groaned to find itself Arian," ("Ingemuit totus orbis et se Arianum esse miratus est"). At Seleucia. in 360 A.D., the result was a semi-Arian Creed, from which the term "Homöousion" was excluded, as being difficult to understand, but the word

---

[15] Cf. Hooker's "Eccles. Pol.," v. xlii., § 5; and Milman's "H. of C.," iii. 5.

"Anomœan," or "unlike," as speaking of the Son in His relation to the Father, was denounced, and at the same time the chief leaders of extreme Arianism were excommunicated.

Athanasius has drawn up an account of the earlier proceedings of these Councils in the form of a *"Letter on the Councils of Ariminum and Seleucia,"* at which Councils it has been supposed though with much improbability, that he himself was present. This treatise of Athanasius is distinguished by the gentler tone which he adopts in speaking of those semi-Arians, whose objections to the Nicene Creed were verbal rather than real.

The Arian controversy, not only made itself felt throughout the Church, but affected the State at the same time, shaking the Roman Empire to its very foundations. It was consequently, perhaps, better on the whole and under the peculiar circumstances of the case, that these views which were so widely prevalent should be thoroughly discussed and ventilated, than that they should have been at once silenced, either by authority or compromise, and thus allowed secretly to fester in the body of the Church. Thus the Church was enabled to secure a form of sound words, which was of the greatest benefit to her in after times of ignorance and darkness. In one sense, therefore, this sad controversy may have been overruled to the good of Christianity.

(2.) It would appear to be now pretty generally admitted that Antioch, and not Alexandria, must be regarded as the original seat or cradle of Arianism. The theological teaching at Antioch was logical, subtle, and refined, not deep or broad. We find Paul of Samosata elevated to the bishopric of that city not long after the martyrdom of Babylas. He was originally a Sophist, and founded a school there. He was patronised by Zenobia;

and introduced into the Church at Antioch all the subtle
and casuistical subjects of inquiry, which were discussed
in the academies of the heathen, advocating himself a
doctrine which was closely akin to Sabellianism. He
exerted a very extensive influence over the educated
classes in the city. Lucian, a presbyter in the same city—
in after times a martyr—had also a school at Antioch,
which enjoyed a high reputation. In that school were
educated some of the most distinguished of the Arian
party. Not only was Arius one of his pupils, but he
claimed also Eusebius of Nicomedia, Eudoxius,
Leontius, and Asterius. They were afterwards called
"Collucianists" (Theod., i. 5; Epiph., "Hæres.," lxix. 6),
from their having studied together under Lucian. Being
accused of holding heterodox views he was
excommunicated, but, about twelve years before his
martyrdom, he was again admitted into the Church. He
received commendation at the hands of Chrysostom,
Rufinus, and Jerome. Thus can we see the *historical*
connexion that existed between the Arians and the
schools of Antioch. Eusebius, the historian, was also in
part educated at Antioch, though not in the school of
Lucian; and so was Paulinus of Tyre. Both were
suspected of holding Arian or semi-Arian views.
Moreover of the bishops who Arianized at the Council
of Nicæa, nine belonged to the Patriarchate of Syria.
Again, from the time of the Nicene Council to the death
of Arius (325–361 A.D.), Antioch was the metropolis of
heresy, as Alexandria was of orthodoxy. Semi-Arianism
was first developed in a Council at Antioch, when
Lucian's Creed was brought forward; and not only were
negotiations respecting Arianism conducted at Antioch
with the Western Church, but also at Antioch and at
Tyre (a suffragan see) a sentence of condemnation was

passed upon Athanasius. It may be observed also, that
the Jews had greatly increased in numbers, and in power
and position at Antioch. Their luxurious and selfish
habits had proved injurious to the growth of true
Christianity in the city. And even before the end of the
first century we can trace the up-growth of the
Cerinthians and Ebionites—both tainted with
Gnosticism—and also of the Nazarenes. And not only
did there exist this connexion between Judaism and
unsoundness of views prior to the age of Paul of
Samosata, but his opinions were decidedly
humanitarian—of Jewish origin—and so was his ritual.
It may also be historically remarked that in the different
tumults and insurrections that took place in favour of
Arianism both at Antioch and Alexandria, the Jews
always sided with the un-orthodox party. And, in proof
of the fact that Arianism had its origin in Antioch, we
may quote the words of Alexander, in his letter to the
Church of Constantinople:—"Ye are not ignorant
concerning Arianism, that this rebellious doctrine
belongs to Ebion and Artemas, and is in imitation of
Paulus of Samosata, Bishop of Antioch, who was
deprived by the sentence of the bishops assembled in
Council from all quarters. Paul was succeeded by
Lucian, who remained in excommunication for many
years during the time of three bishops…. Our present
heretics have drunk up the dregs of their impiety, and
are their secret offspring" (cf. "The Arians," 27).

(3.) The singularly rapid up-growth of Arianism is
justly referred to as a striking feature in connexion with
its history. Within the short space of six years it required
the interposition of a General Council. Although it was
there condemned by almost all the bishops who were
present, it soon again started into prominence. Not only

did it win for itself the support of the palace, but it also seized upon the most exalted posts of dignity in the Church, and occupied the chair at Councils, and trampled on the necks of the orthodox. We can scarcely doubt that one of the principal reasons to be adduced for this remarkable success may be discovered in the fact of the great influence which those who were educated under Lucian had acquired. They filled many of the most important positions in the Church at that time.

Moreover, it is generally acknowledged, that in almost every conflict, the attacking party has a decided advantage over those who are attacked. The weaker and more vulnerable side of the party assailed may thus be made the object of assault. It was by the adoption of this artifice, that Arianism was in the first place successful. In addition to this, it was indebted for its success to the fact of its being a sceptical rather than a dogmatic system; to its being destructive rather than constructive. Its ostensible object was to inquire into and reform the received Creed, and not to hazard one of its own. Heresies which had preceded it had made profession of a formulary of belief, and so had fallen. Such had been the fate of the Gnostic system. But the Antiochene school took the ground of an assailant. And, consequently, when Arianism was itself arraigned, and placed on the defensive before the Nicene Council, and when afterwards it began to occupy the chairs of Theology, it split into different factions and gave way.

(4.) Theodosius the Great, carefully brought up in the Nicene faith, convened, after his victory over the Goths, the second Œcumenical Council of Constantinople in 381 A.D. During his distinguished reign the triumph of orthodoxy over Arianism was effected, and the orthodox doctrine of the Holy Trinity firmly established by a decree of the above-named Council. Arianism, as a systematic motive-power in theology and Church history, then ceased to exist under imperial rule. But the ecclesiastical legislation of Theodosius was naturally confined to the boundaries of the Roman Empire. Beyond that limit the Gothic tribes, who had received Christianity under an Arian dress in the days of Valens, still continued for nearly two hundred years—more, perhaps, from the force of habit, than the dictates of a theological or intellectual conviction—to embrace the tenets of Arianism. It became the distinctive creed of the barbarian tribes that overran the Roman Empire. As we have already seen (ch. vi. p. 57), Alaric, who conquered Rome, and Genseric, who subdued North Africa, were imbued with the teaching of Arius. The same may be said of Theodoric the Great, the king of Italy. The Vandals, who subjugated the North of Africa in 429 A.D., and grievously and cruelly persecuted the orthodox in that region, were under Arian influence till 530 A.D. The Ostrogoths maintained Arian views till 553 A.D.; the Visigoths were under the same theological influence until the Council of Toledo, nearly fifty years later; and the Suevi in Spain till the year 560 A.D. The Burgundians also remained Arians till they were incorporated in 534 A.D. in the Frank Empire; and the Langobardi in Italy held these same views, even down to the middle of the 7th century.

Of all the wild and war-loving hosts that swept, like an overwhelming torrent, over the length and breadth of the dominions that owned the sway of Rome, the Goths were the most famous. The seeds of Christianity would seem to have been first planted among them by the Christian captives whom they carried off to Dacia and the neighbourhood of the Danube; but the great work of evangelizing these wild warriors was chiefly carried on by the efforts of Ulphilas, who was both a missionary and a bishop among them. He was a professed advocate, indeed, of the doctrine of Arius, and was said to have signed the Creed of Ariminum; but he was a man of earnest zeal, of blameless walk, and of truth and piety. He not only acted as a missionary amongst them, but also executed the difficult work of translating portions of the Holy Scriptures into the tongue of those amongst whom he laboured, which was a dialect of the German or Teutonic language. To compose such a version—parts of which are still extant—was a hard task; and it is said that he was compelled to form a new alphabet—named the Mæso-Gothic alphabet, in order to express the peculiar sounds which were foreign to either Greek or Latin pronunciation.

It has been remarked by Gibbon (ch. xxxvii.) that the Visigoths also embraced the Christian faith, and taught their children the truths of Christianity, and that "in their long and victorious march from the Danube to the Atlantic Ocean, the devotion which reigned in the camp of Attila, or the Court of Toulouse, might edify or disgrace the palaces of Rome and Constantinople."

What the precise motives may have been that induced the Gothic tribes to embrace the religion of Christ—deeply interesting though the inquiry may be—we cannot now investigate. We know, however, that the effects and consequences which followed upon their conversion were of the most beneficial character on their religious, social, and intellectual condition. But, unhappily, these good effects were, to a certain extent, marred by the peculiar form of religious belief under which Christianity was presented to them—the form of Arianism.

(5.) Arianism was, it would seem, closely connected in its philosophical relations with the Aristotelic school, and also with the schools of the Sophists. Such is the view maintained by the author of "The Arians," and by Baur, though some critics have endeavoured to trace its connexion, with less plausibility, to the school of Plato. Arius himself was an adept in sophistical disputation; Paul of Samosata was branded as a Sophist; Asterius had been a Sophist by profession; Aetius was trained in the school of an Alexandrian Aristotelian, and Eunomius, his pupil, was, according to Rufinus, remarkable for his dialectical proficiency. And hence, even in that century, Aristotle was designated the "Bishop of the Arians." Of this logical, and empirical, and dialectical tendency of Arianism, Basil and the Gregories, as well as Ambrose and Cyril, loudly complain. Such dialectical exercises were obviously open to abuse, though moderated by ever so orthodox and strictly Scriptural a rule, in an age when no sufficient ecclesiastical symbol existed, as a guide to the memory and judgment of the eager disputant.

"Aiming (says Epiphanius, "Hæres.," 809) to exhibit the Divine nature by means of Aristotelic syllogisms and geometrical data, they are naturally led on to declare that Christ is not the very Son of God."

(6.) An imaginary rather than real affinity between the eclectic doctrine on the subject of the Trinity, and that which was held by the Arian school, has induced many to believe that Arianism was first introduced into the Church through members of the Church of Alexandria.

It would seem, however, that Arianism, though openly developed in the first instance at Alexandria, was only developed there from accidental circumstances. We do not find that any one of eminence in the city backed it up by his influence or authority; but that, on the contrary, it was driven from the Church together with its promoter. Nor is there any proof that the older Platonism had any part in the origination of the Arian doctrine; nor, indeed, can neo-Platonism be charged with having favoured it at its first promulgation. And though we admit that some of the Alexandrian Fathers have employed terms which resemble those which were afterwards used by Arian writers, it was only after all an accidental resemblance that can be traced between them. The writers of that day referred its origin to Judaism, and especially to the teaching of the Sophists. Thus, as we have already noticed, Alexander ascribes its origin to Antioch; tracing up its history to Judaism; to the love of disputation that existed, and to the fact that Arius and his party were closely connected with the school of Antioch.

(7.) We learn definitely from Scripture not only the divinity of Christ, but also His personal distinction from God. This is stated with sufficient clearness in the commencement of the Gospel of St. John, as clearly, indeed, as any formulary of the Church could state it.

It has been rightly asserted that the whole doctrine turns on the two following truths, namely, that "our Lord is one with, yet personally separate from, God," and thus there are two titles given to Him in Holy Scripture, which enforce respectively these two essential features of the orthodox doctrine; imperfect, indeed, in themselves, and liable to be misunderstood, but qualifying and completing one another. Thus "the title of the *Son* marks His derivation and distinction from the Father; that of *Word* (*i.e.*, Reason) denotes His inseparable inherence in the Divine Unity; and while the former, taken by itself, might lead one to conceive of Him as a second being, and the latter as no real being at all, both together witness to the mystery, that He is at once *from*, and yet *in*, the Immaterial, Incomprehensible God." Athanasius ("De Syn.," 41) says, "The Son is the Word and Wisdom of the Father; from which titles we infer His *spiritual* and *indivisible* derivation from the Father, inasmuch as the Word (or Reason) of a man is no part of him, nor when exercised, implies any change in the immaterial principle; much less, therefore, is it so with the Word of God. On the other hand, the Father calls Him His Son, lest from hearing only that He was the Word, we should fail to consider Him as *real;* whereas the title of Son designates Him as an *existing* Word, and a *substantial* Wisdom."

It would seem evident that, until the time of Irenæus, the Godhead of the Father, Son, and Holy Ghost, had been maintained with such earnestness and tenacity on the part of Christians, that there was no danger lest the language employed might seem to savour of Sabellianism. When such a tendency exhibited itself, it was sufficient at that time to affirm with greater clearness the distinction existing between the Persons of the blessed Godhead. It was now, however, in the fourth century, necessary to reconcile together the great truths which were involved in the controversy, and to form them into a consistent whole.

The terms (so Canon Robertson has remarked, "Ch. Hist.," ii. 1) by which the relations of the Divine Being had been expressed, were intended to be regarded as complementary of each other in conveying such a shadow of the mystery as is within the compass of human thought and language; and, if taken singly, they were liable to be misunderstood. When the matter is thus regarded, we can see that the term "Son" was, when strictly considered, an imperfect mode of expressing the relations subsisting between the First and Second Persons of the Trinity, because, though it implied the derivation of very God from very God, and the identity of nature, it seemed, nevertheless, to suggest the notion of "posteriority, inferiority, and material generation." While, on the contrary, the term "Word" or "Reason" (Logos) conveyed the ideas of "coeternity, essential indwelling, and mediation, but tended to obscure that of personality, rather suggesting that the Second Person was to the First as an attribute or a mode of operation." On such incompleteness in the images employed to represent the relations of the Divine Being, it has been supposed that Arius founded his heretical doctrines.

Logic or dialectics was the great instrument that Arius employed. He was not a philosopher or a metaphysician. His mind dwelt on terms rather than on ideas. The difficulty of fully understanding his principles and his Creed is increased by the fact that he was continually altering and shifting his views, sometimes by the endeavour to extricate himself from the logical results of his theories, which he had not himself foreseen; and, at other times, from the desire to disguise his sentiments from those, to whom their bald and naked statement might cause estrangement, and destroy all sympathy with him. His terrible doctrine respecting the mutability of the Son's will, and, as a consequence, of His liability to fall, he would seem in the end to have retracted.

(8.) It has been remarked of some of the semi-Arian party, that "the men were better than their Creed." And there is truth in the statement. For although a large proportion of the Arianizing party were worldly and irreligious, yet it must be confessed that many of the semi-Arians were men of piety and of blameless lives, which marked them off with great clearness from the Eusebians, who made no concealment of their devotion to the maxims and practices of the world. And thus it was that such men as Athanasius and Hilary were ready to allow their claim to the privilege of private Christian fellowship, though they deemed it right for the edification and well-being of the Church at large, that the doctrine of the "Homöousion" should be upheld and maintained. They could not withhold such fellowship from Basil, whose life was blameless and whose learning was vast; or from Eustathius of Sebaste; or from Eleusius of Cyzicus—men whom Hilary characterises as most holy—"Sanctissimi viri;" and even Mark of Arethusa, violent as he was, has received from Gregory Nazianzen and Theodoret commendation for his zeal in making converts, and for his piety and intellectual qualifications; while Cyril of Jerusalem, though a semi-Arian, has won fame for the eloquence and beauty of his addresses to the catechumens of his Church.

(9.) The Arians endeavoured to maintain the doctrines which they put forward by a reference to passages in the Bible in which Christ would, superficially, appear to be placed on a level with the creature—passages which, in their bearing on this controversy, Athanasius has referred to and explained in his different writings.

Arianism, however—such is Dr. Schaff's assertion— was "refuted by an array of Scripture passages which teach, directly or indirectly, the Divinity of Christ, and His equality with the Father. Its conception of a created Creator, who existed before the world, and yet Himself began to exist, was shown to be self-contradictory and untenable. There can be no middle being between Creator and creature; no time before the world, as time is itself part of the world, or the form under which it exists successively; nor can the unchangeableness of the Father, on which Arius laid great stress, be maintained, except on the ground of the eternity of His Fatherhood, which, of course, implies the eternity of the Son-ship."

"The sneer of Gibbon (it has been well said by Canon Liddon, 'Bampt. Lect.' vii.) about the iota which separates the semi-Arian from the Catholic symbol ('Homoiousion' from 'Homöousion') is naturally repeated by those who believe that nothing was really at stake beyond the emptiest of abstractions, and who can speak of the fourth century as an age of meaningless logomachies. But to men who are concerned, not with words, but with the truths which they enshrine, not with the mere historic setting of a great struggle, but with the vital question at issue in it, the full importance of the Nicene symbol will be sufficiently obvious. The difference between 'Homoiousion' and 'Homöousion' convulsed the world for the simple reason, that in that difference lay the whole question of the real truth or falsehood of our Lord's actual Divinity. If in His Essence He was only like God, He was still a distinct Being from God, and therefore either created, or (*per impossibile*) a Second God.... Certainly (he eloquently adds), if toil and suffering confer a value on the object which they earn or preserve; if a country prizes the liberties which were baptized in the blood of her citizens; if a man rejoices in the honour which he has kept unstained at the risk of life; then we, who are the heirs of the ages of Christendom, should cling with a peculiar loyalty and love to the great Nicene Confession of our Lord's Divinity. For the Nicene definition was wrung from the heart of the agonized Church by a denial of the truth on which was fed, then as now, her inmost life. In the Arian heresy the old enemies of the Gospel converged as for a final and desperate effort to achieve its destruction. At this day the Creed of Nicæa is the living proof of the Church's victory; and as we confess it we should, methinks, feel somewhat of the fire of our spiritual ancestors, some measure of that fresh glow of thankfulness, which is due to God after a great deliverance, although wrought out in a distant age."

www.ingramcontent.com/pod-product-compliance
Lightning Source LLC
Chambersburg PA
CBHW071601150726
48000CB00004B/1550